WILLETRUDIS
VERSES ABOUT SUSANNA

Latin Text with
Running Vocabulary and Commentary

THE **EXPERRECTA** SERIES

Women Latin Authors

Pixelia Senior Editors:

Caedmon Haas

Thomas G. Hendrickson

John T. Lanier

Anna C. Pisarello

Ben Wiebracht

All titles available open access at pixeliapublishing.org

WILLETRUDIS
VERSES ABOUT SUSANNA

Latin Text with
Running Vocabulary and Commentary

Edited, with introduction and notes, by

Abbe Walker
Merlin Gouesse
Lauren Kelley
Emmeline Murphy
Natalie Peterson
Sophie Pong
Grace Richards
Isabel Tolman-Bronski
Charles Drew White

PIXELIA PUBLISHING

Title: Willetrudis. Verses about Susanna

Subtitle: Latin Text with Running Vocabulary and Commentary

First Edition

Copyright © 2026 Pixelia Publishing

ISBN (paperback): 978-1-967785-09-4
ISBN (ebook): 978-1-967785-10-0

Published May 2026 by Pixelia Publishing (pixeliapublishing.org)

Cover design by John Lanier

Font: Cardo, an open source font in the Google Fonts collection, designed by David Perry

<u>Front Cover</u>: detail from Cecil Buller, *Susanna and the Elders*, 1920-1929. Linocut in black on ivory Japanese paper. Smithsonian American Art Museum 1976.134.

CONTENTS

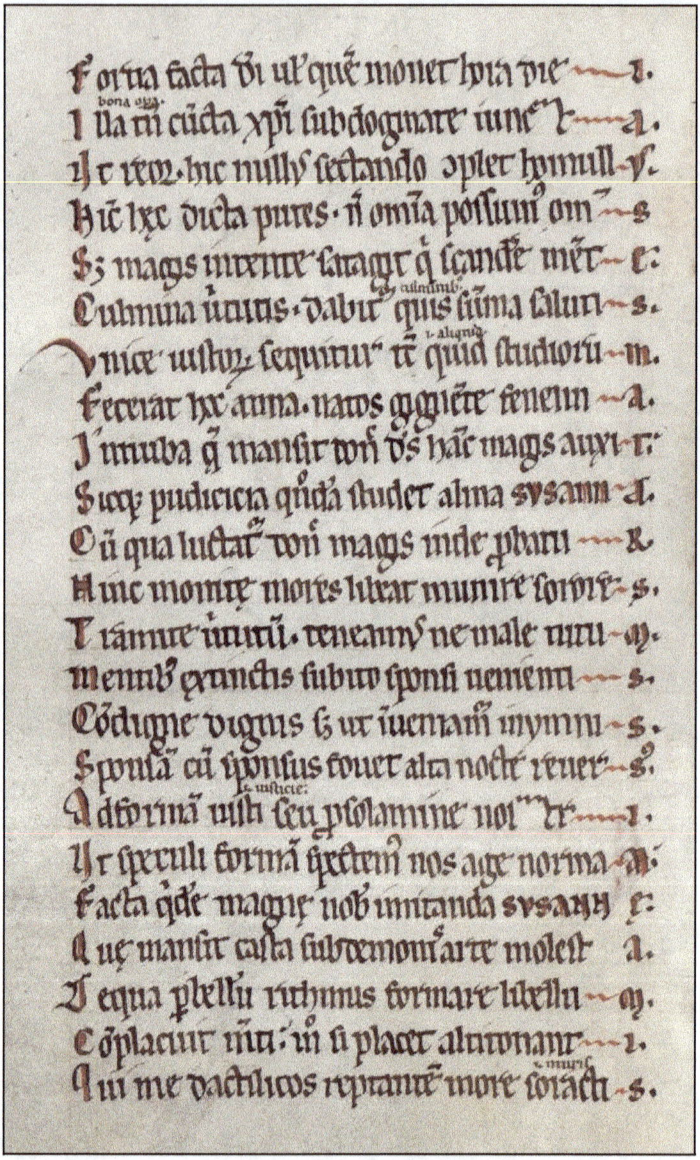

Figure 1. A page from the sole extant manuscript of Willetrudis' *dē Sūsannā*, Bayerische Staatsbibliothek München, Clm 12513 (f. 23v).

Acknowledgments

This project was inspired by scholars dedicated to new and collaborative pedagogical models that help make the Latin language more engaging and accessible to students. In particular, we would like to thank Tom Hendrickson at Pixelia, who provided the initial inspiration and guidance at all stages of the process. Additionally, we would like to thankCaedmon Haas, John Lanier, Christy Marquis, Anna Pisarello, and Ben Wiebracht for all their support and valuable feedback.

Thank you to the Department of Classics at Northwestern, especially Francesca Tataranni, for encouraging the project from the beginning. We would also like to thank Richard Kieckhefer for giving us a thorough crash course in Latin paleography, and Bret Mulligan at Haverford College for his help in creating our vocabulary list.

Special thanks to all the scholars bringing Latin written by women to light. In addition to all the contributors and editors of the Experrecta series, we would like to express our gratitude to Jane Stevenson (*Women Latin Poets*) and Skye Shirley (www.lupercallegit.org/) for drawing our attention and curiosity to the poet Willetrudis.

Finally, we would like to thank the many friends, family members, and colleagues who helped and supported us in the creation of this commentary. Grātiās vōbīs agimus!

ABOUT THE AUTHORS

Joint authorship is uncommon in the humanities. As a byline with nine names might well prompt questions, we wanted to say a few words about our methods.

This commentary is the result of a collaborative project initiated in an advanced Latin course on women's Latin at Northwestern University in Spring 2024 taught by Professor Abbe Walker. The course design was inspired by Tom Hendrickson's model for collaborative commentary building.

The student editors of this edition were Merlin Gouesse, Lauren Kelley, Emmeline Murphy, Natalie Peterson, Sophie Pong, Grace Richards, Isabel Tolman-Bronski, and Charles Drew White. Each student acted as section editor of one portion of the poem. The project unfolded in five stages. First, students used scans of the manuscript, which is digitized online, paired with Silagi's 1999 edition, to transcribe their sections into a shared document. Richard Kieckhefer, professor emeritus of Religious Studies at Northwestern, ran a workshop on paleography to enable students to work more closely with the manuscript. Next, students added macrons to their transcriptions using a Latin Macronizer[1] and then checking its work against lexica like those available on Logeion[2] and our own scansion of the Leonine hexameters.

---

[1] alatius.com/macronizer/

[2] logeion.uchicago.edu

Using The Bridge's Lemmatizer,[3] we created a shared lemmatization spreadsheet to build the vocabulary list. Students edited their own sections and refined definitions that could be specific to a medieval text using the *Dictionary of Medieval Latin from British Sources* available on Logeion. We refined our on-page vocabulary further by removing the top 500 Latin words based on the Dickinson College Commentaries Latin Core vocabulary list and placing those words in a final glossary at the back of the book. Students worked on translations of their sections throughout the course, and they workshopped these translations during class. Students then prepared the on-page comments based on our class discussions. Finally, each student wrote a portion of the introduction.

After the course, Professor Walker, Isabel Tolman-Bronski, and Natalie Peterson completed the portions of the poem for which there were no section editors during the course. They edited the whole commentary for tone and consistency, and Professor Walker edited and wrote portions of the introduction.

---

[3] bridge.haverford.edu

About the Experrecta Series

Women have written a substantial amount of Latin literature, but there are very few editions of that literature geared towards student use. The goal of the Experrecta series is to create student editions of Latin texts written by women. The aim of each edition is to assist students in reading the works of these authors in the original Latin. To that end, each edition will include help with the author's vocabulary and grammar, as well as an introduction to provide historical background on her life and works. The name of the series comes from Vibia Perpetua, who was among the first women to write a surviving work in Latin. In her narrative, Perpetua recounts a series of visions, each of which ends with the phrase *Et experrēcta sum* ("And I awoke"). This series will be populated by texts that have long been slumbering and are now waking to a new dawn and a new readership in Latin classrooms.

IMAGES

INTRODUCTION

I. THE PURPOSE OF THIS EDITION

Tucked away in a lone medieval manuscript in Munich lies a story
of corrupt lust, steadfast virtue, and divine vindication. That text is
Willetrudis' *dē Sūsannā*, a retelling of the story of Susanna—a
married woman falsely accused of adultery after rejecting the
sexual advances of two powerful judges—as told in Daniel 13.
Willetrudis' version, however, is more than just a retelling of a
familiar biblical tale. As the only known Latin treatment of the
story of Susanna authored by a woman—a *scrīptrīx*, as Willetrudis
calls herself (line 369)—it is a valuable witness to a woman's
literary voice in the medieval period. In choosing this tale,
Willetrudis created something distinctive: a woman's reworking of
scripture about a female exemplar of virtue, addressed to her
sorōrēs, her fellow nuns, within the literate world of a women's
convent. That is, with *dē Sūsannā*, we have a Latin poem written
by a woman, about a woman, for women.

Yet the centuries during which this neglected work gathered dust
also remind us how often women's contributions to Latin
literature have been overlooked, undervalued, or rendered
invisible within the broader literary tradition. Surveys and
compendia of Latin literature tend to highlight the contributions
of just a few token women, framing them as isolated examples
rather than as participants in a wider culture of female Latin
authorship. In reality, women were active contributors to the
Latin tradition across periods. As the authors of one recent

anthology put it, "Latin was a language of women as well as of men."[1] Nevertheless, the precarious survival of their work—threatened by manuscript loss, dispersal, anonymous attribution, or neglect—has contributed to the impression that women's Latin was marginal, anomalous, or of lesser value.

Of course, women in all periods did face unique barriers to Latin authorship. Within Willetrudis' medieval context, those who could read and write Latin were an elite within an elite. Latin was a language of the highly educated and powerful, particularly associated with those trained in the burgeoning universities of the Middle Ages, which excluded women as students.[2] Jan Ziolkowski has observed:

> The best way to conceive of Latin in the Middle Ages may be as a *father tongue*. This description conveys Latin's special quality as a language spoken by no one as a mother tongue. Furthermore, it hints at the status of Latin as a mainly male language, since most of the people who had the opportunity to learn Latin were boys and men…who occupied posts within a strongly patriarchal system.[3]

Despite this apparent male monopoly on the Latin language, convents in particular could sustain vibrant literary communities of women reading and writing in Latin. Against this background,

---

[1] Churchill, Brown, and Jeffrey 2002: 1. Women's authorship has increasingly become an area of focus for scholars of Latin literature. In addition to Churchill, Brown, and Jeffrey 2002, see also Stevenson 2005a and 2005b, Dronke 1984, Thiébaux 1994, Natoli, Pitts, and Hallett 2022, and Watt 2020.
[2] Stevenson 2005a: 109.
[3] Ziolkowski 1996: 506.

Willetrudis emerges as a crucial voice. If, as Jane Stevenson has suggested (as discussed below), she is the Willetrudis of Wilton, her poem offers us a rare glimpse into one of the most learned convents of medieval England, situating her within a broader female intellectual milieu. Her Latin is ambitious and stylistically bold, engaging with the so-called "hermeneutic style" popular in early medieval England, which shows both her awareness of and participation in contemporary literary traditions.[4] Additionally, her choice of Susanna as subject places her in dialogue with other verse retellings by her male contemporaries, who were influenced by a tradition that represented Susanna's beauty as a trap for the male gaze and a danger to herself.[5] Willetrudis' Susanna, by contrast, emerges as "an ideal of active and heroic womanhood," a model for both nuns and lay women, and the corrupt elders of her story are sharply exposed in their abuse of power.[6] Willetrudis' use of the Latin "father tongue" to tell a story about a woman for women is thus doubly striking: it shows her entering a tradition coded as male, and yet reshaping it to center female virtue and expose male corruption.

Our primary goals in creating this edition have been to recover the voice of a woman writer in a male-dominated literary tradition and render it accessible to a modern audience. Though Willetrudis' *dē Sūsannā* represents a significant contribution to medieval Latin literature, it survives in only one medieval manuscript. Until now, it has only been available in an article in

---

[4] For more on the "hermeneutic style," see Lapidge 1975.

[5] Stevenson 2005a: 131. For more on medieval narratives depicting women as temptresses or traps for men, see Bloch 1991.

[6] Stevenson 2005a: 136.

an academic journal, which provides the bare text with footnotes focused primarily on identifying places where Willetrudis most closely borrows from the Vulgate version of Daniel 13, as well as the Latin text of the marginalia found in the manuscript.[7] The article provides no comprehensive vocabulary or grammatical aid.[8] Additionally, the poem has never been translated into English or any other language.

Our edition provides, for the first time, an accessible Latin text with vocabulary, commentary, and a full English translation. Our vocabulary and grammatical aids aim to demystify Willetrudis' complex Latin, allowing learners to engage with post-Classical Latin in classrooms or independently. The value of this edition lies not only in making Willetrudis' poem newly available, but also in ensuring that it can be read, taught, and studied by audiences ranging from undergraduate students to seasoned scholars.

II. SUSANNA AND THE ELDERS

To appreciate more fully what Willetrudis accomplishes in her retelling, it is important to first recall the original story of Susanna and trace the journey of its subsequent reception.

---

[7] Silagi 1999.

[8] Silagi (1999) does provide a short but useful introduction discussing the manuscript, some of the idiosyncrasies of Willetrudis' Latin, and her classical references. Nevertheless, the introduction, and all of Silagi's footnotes, are in German, making it inaccessible to many students.

Biblical Background

The story unfolds during the Babylonian exile in the 6th century BCE. Susanna is the virtuous wife of a wealthy man named Joachim. Because of his wealth and standing in the community, Joachim's house in Babylon has become a gathering place for the exiled Jewish community to deliberate on legal matters. Among the frequent visitors to the house are two elders, recently appointed as judges. Inflamed with passion by Susanna's beauty, the two elders hatch a plan to proposition her for sex as soon as they can catch her in a compromised position. It is Susanna's regular daily habit to enjoy the private garden adjacent to her house, and on one very hot day, she orders her servants to lock the garden gates so she can bathe in the fountain, unaware that the elders have hidden themselves inside to spy on her. Seeing their opportunity, they ambush her, insisting that she have sex with them. Should she refuse, they threaten to defame her by saying they caught her under a tree in the arms of a lover—a capital offense. Susanna chooses to risk death rather than surrender to their sinful demands, trusting that her innocence will be transparent to God. At her trial the next day, the elders, full of false indignation, tell their fabricated story. Her community, torn between respect for her renowned chastity and deference to the elders, ultimately condemn her to death. In response to her fervent prayers, God intervenes via his young prophet Daniel. Daniel challenges the verdict and insists on interrogating each elder separately, specifically asking under which type of tree they caught Susanna and her alleged lover. When each gives a different answer, Daniel exposes them as liars and saves Susanna from her imminent execution. The reversal is completed, and justice is finally served, when the elders receive the very punishment they had intended for Susanna.

The basic story first appears as the 13th chapter of the Book of Daniel in the Septuagint, which was the earliest translation of the Hebrew Bible (also known as the Old Testament). The translation, from Hebrew into Greek, was initiated in Alexandria, Egypt, in the 3rd century BCE and completed around the end of the 2nd century BCE. The story's pre-Septuagint form is a matter of conjecture. The episode does not appear in any Hebrew versions of Daniel and has never been considered canonical by Jews.[9] Lorenzo DiTommoso argues that it is one of a collection of apocryphal episodes that were added to the canonical book of Daniel that reached its final form around 164 BCE.[10] While some scholars have posited a now-lost original "extra-biblical" text written in Aramaic or another Semitic language meant to highlight Daniel's prophetic powers, Carey Moore, among others, has suggested the episode was originally a secular folktale later adapted to a Jewish context.[11]

If Carey is right, then the Septuagint recorded a tale that had already evolved considerably, and indeed, creative adaptation and interpretation continued to define the Susanna story from the

---

[9] While Catholic and Orthodox churches consider Daniel 13 canonical, Protestant denominations, following the Hebrew canon, classify it as apocryphal.
[10] DiTommaso 2005: 3.
[11] Moore (1977: 88–89) notes that the story features two prominent folk tale motifs: "(1) the wise judge; and (2) the 'Genoveva' theme, i.e., 'the widespread tale of the chaste wife falsely accused and repudiated, generally on the word of a rejected suitor.'"

second century CE until well beyond the 17th century.[12] In the second century CE, Theodotion, a Hellenistic Jewish scholar perhaps living in Ephesus, created a new Greek translation of Daniel that came to be the one preferred by the early Christian church, fully replacing the older Septuagint version.[13] Theodotion's version reshaped the Susanna story into a more dramatic tale, less about community justice and more about the interplay between beauty, lust, and piety. In this version, Theodotion introduced the bathing scene, which had been totally absent from the Septuagint, and added clauses emphasizing Susanna's beauty and vulnerability. As Halpern-Amaru notes, Theodotion's changes—from heightening the heroes and villains to erasing the Jewish communal setting of the synagogue—proved decisive for a Christian audience eager to use the story in its developing effort at self-definition.[14]

Reception Among Early Christian Authors
Theodotion's reshaping of the tale set the stage for early Christian authors, who drew upon Susanna not only as a story of divine

---

[12] For an overview of the origins, adaptations, and interpretations of the Susanna story, see Spolsky 1996a.

[13] In the Prologue to his commentary on Daniel (*Commentārium in Daniēlem*), the 4th century CE theologian Jerome mentions that Theodotion's revised version was the one read in churches: "The churches of the Lord Savior do not read the prophet Daniel according to the Seventy Interpreters [i.e., the Septuagint], using the edition of Theodotion; and why this happened I do not know" (translation by Moore [1977: 31]). Only two manuscripts, unpublished until 1772, preserve the Septuagint version (Moore 1977: 16n25). The identity of Theodotion is uncertain. Irenaeus (*Adversus Haeresēs* 3.21.1) mentions a Theodotion of Ephesus, but Moore argues that this is not the same person who translated or edited the later version of Daniel (1977: 16-17, 31).

[14] Halpern-Amaru 1996: 24.

vindication but also as a *locus* for debates about gender and sexuality. Ambrose, bishop of Milan from 374 CE, praises Susanna's silence and unwillingness to protest her innocence to anyone but God as a sure sign of modesty, the companion and guardian of chastity.[15]

Figure 2. Detail of Susanna and the Elders, fresco from the Catacombs of Priscilla, Rome, fourth century CE. Wilpert 1903, Tav. 14.

---

[15] *Dē officiīs clēricōrum* 1.18.

Tertullian (160-c. 225 CE) emphasizes Susanna's modesty and innocence expressed in her use of the veil, which concealed her beauty from view, warning that unveiled women exposed themselves to danger and disgrace.[16] Among authors like Clement of Alexandria (150-c. 215 CE), Novatian (c. 200-c. 258), and Augustine (354-430 CE), Susanna became an important model for married women's fidelity during times of heated debate within the early Christian church about the status of married versus virginal or celibate Christians.[17]

Early Christian art reflects a similar preoccupation with Susanna's propriety and modesty over her ordeal. The earliest images depicting Susanna are found in the so-called "Greek Chapel" of the Catacombs of Priscilla in Rome, dated to the mid-third century CE. In one of the three scenes telling her story, Susanna appears fully clothed and veiled, with her arms and eyes uplifted to God in the traditional posture of prayer, while the elders are focused on her, reaching out in an attempt to touch her body. In a second scene, the elders hold down her arms from prayer as they lay their hands upon her, a gesture that both refers to their judicial accusation and alludes to their own preoccupation with sensual touch (see Figure 2).

---

[16] *Dē corōnā* 4.3. In his treatise *On the Veiling of Virgins*, he does not mention Susanna by name, but he is even more explicit in his warning that an unveiled woman exposes herself to danger, "it is inevitable that, by the public exposure of herself, she is imperiled, as she is struck by countless and untrustworthy eyes" (*necesse est pūblicātiōne suī perīclitētur, dum percutitur oculīs incertīs et multīs, Dē virginibus velāndīs* 14 [PL 2, col. 909 B]).

[17] For an overview of the use and interpretations of Susanna's story in patristic literature see: Halpern-Amaru 1996, Smith 1993, and de Wet 2009.

Images of Susanna also appear on sarcophagi from the fourth century CE. In one example in the Musée de l'Art Chrétien in Arles, Susanna holds an open scroll directed toward the viewer. Smith argues that the scroll, a symbol of wisdom and social status on both Christian and non-Christian sarcophagi, serves as a proof of the status of Susanna's spiritual purity externalized for the viewer to confirm (see Figure 3).[18]

Figure 3. Detail of "Susanna" sarcophagus, found near Arles, c. 350 CE. Musée de l'Art Chrétien, Arles / ArtStor.

Reception Among Medieval Authors

Medieval writers inherited and expanded these interpretive traditions. Peter Abelard (1079-1142), Alan of Melsa (1204-1212), and Peter Riga (1140-1209) all use Susanna's story to urge women to guard their virtue, reflecting a patriarchal tendency to associate the preservation of chastity with female conduct.[19] For Abelard, writing to the nuns of the Paraclete, Susanna instructs the sisters that chastity is not guaranteed by their vows or sequestered lives,

---

[18] Smith 1993: 15-16

[19] For the reception of the story of Susanna in medieval sources, see Jeffrey 1996, McAvoy 2021 (esp. 286-329), Mozley 1930, Staley 2007, and Stevenson 2005a (esp. 131-132).

and therefore must be carefully guarded and protected, both from the dangers posed by the outside world and those from within, that is, their pride in their own chastity.[20] The Cistercian monk Alan of Melsa compares Susanna to Penelope, the ancient paradigm of marital fidelity, only to point out that such perfect chastity does not protect a woman from slander.[21] All women, but particularly beautiful women like Susanna, are "never free from jealous suspicion" (*nunquam zēlotipā suspīciōne caret,* 68).

Figure 4. Guercino, *Susanna and the Elders,* 1617.
Museo del Prado, Madrid / ArtStor.

---

[20] *Sermō 29, dē Sānctā Susannā, ad Hortātiōnem Virginum.* See McAvoy (2021: 286-293).
[21] *Tractatus Metricus dē Susannā* 69-70. See Mozley (1930: 41-50) for the Latin text of the poem.

Figure 5. Francesco Hayez, *Susanna at her Bath*, 1850. National Gallery, London.

Peter Riga, a canon of Rheims, especially builds on Theodotion's addition of the bathing scene, dwelling on Susanna's beauty—"her milky neck, her golden hair, her nude flesh" (*cervīx / lactea, cesariēs aurea, nūda carō*, 147-48)—as the spying elders become inflamed with desire.[22] Though he condemns them for their grotesque lust, he implicitly mitigates their crime by depicting them as ensnared by the seductiveness of her body. Female beauty becomes the catalyst for male sin. As Stevenson observes, such versions reflect "the unconscious biases of a medieval man tackling this story."[23]

Figure 6. Jacopo Robusti, called Tintoretto, *Susanna at the Bath*, c.1555-56. Kunsthistorisches Museum Wien / ArtStor.

Artists of the Renaissance, Baroque, and Romantic periods exploited this eroticization of Susanna, typically depicting Susanna nude, often with the attributes of the goddess Venus (e.g., mirrors,

---

[22] This line comes from a poem derived from Riga's Susanna poem (associated with his *Aurora*), later recast into a verse narrative, perhaps by Gilles de Paris (c. 1160-1223/1224), that circulated with the *Aurora* in some manuscripts. Mozley (1930: 36-41) reprints the text from Harley MS 747 (British Library).

[23] Stevenson 2005a: 132.

jewels, and cupids), and positioned to align the viewer with the voyeuristic elders (see Figures 4-6).[24]

Notably, Susanna was also depicted several times by the Italian Baroque artist Artemisia Gentileschi. While her earliest version, painted in 1610, depicts a nude Susanna, participating to a certain extent in the tradition of eroticizing Susanna, this depiction differs markedly from that of her male counterparts (see Figure 6). Gentileschi's Susanna is visibly uncomfortable as she twists her body away from the elders who loom over her threateningly, inviting the viewer to focus on the emotional distress and disgust of Susanna in this moment. In this gesture of active resistance, Gentileschi's Susanna finds a parallel in Willetrudis' Susanna.

Willetrudis' Adaptation

For a community of nuns, the figure of Susanna would have resonated in ways that go beyond an apparent focus on marital chastity or beauty as a snare for male lust. In her prologue, Willetrudis explicitly situates Susanna as a paradigm of female virtue whose story is meant to fortify the monastic community, transforming it from a tale used to regulate women's behavior into one that empowers women through shared spiritual struggle. The story resembles martyrdom accounts, in which virginal saints suffer false or unjust accusations and face death with faithful endurance. Willetrudis herself underscores this parallel when she describes Susanna's near execution as her martyrdom (*martyrium*, 238) and Susanna herself as a great martyr (*martiris…magnae*, 359).

---

[24] For more on Susanna in European paintings, see Spolsky 1996b.

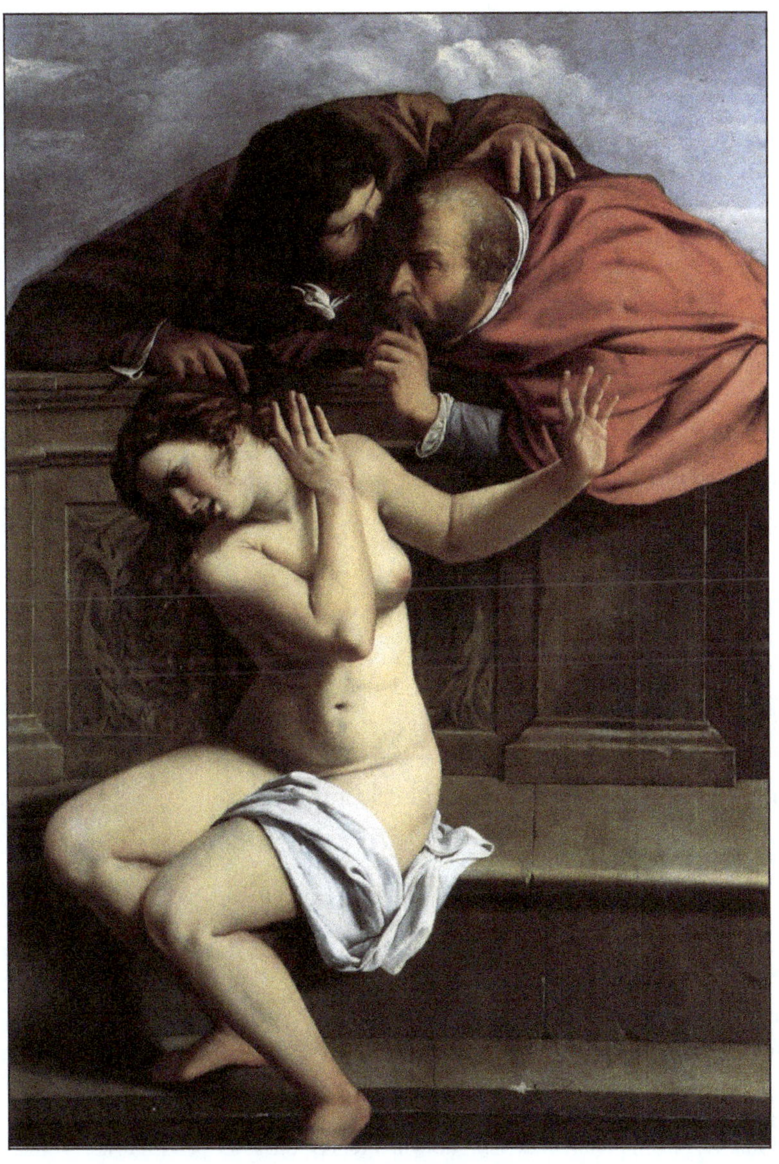

Figure 7. Artemisia Gentileschi, *Susanna and the Elders,* 1610.
Schloss Weißenstein, Pommersfelden / ArtStor.

The story also emphasizes Susanna's unwavering reliance on God's judgment over all others, an especially poignant theme for women whose public standing could mean the survival or dissolution of their community. As Stevenson notes, "calumny could be a serious problem for them [i.e., nuns]. Libel against nuns and proceedings against unsatisfactory convents often resulted in the eviction of the women and their replacement by men—perhaps not always justly."[25] Willetrudis' Susanna provides a model of endurance and faith under pressure.

The main body of the poem follows the Vulgate closely but adds key interpretive elements that subtly but powerfully reshape the narrative.[26] The bathing scene, so often exploited by male interpreters to heighten Susanna's beauty and vulnerability, receives a dramatically different treatment. Willetrudis describes Susanna's beauty only briefly, likening her to a blooming lily, a symbol of virtue and purity, as well as the meaning of her name (48-49, 59-60). In another salient departure, the elders' lechery is not provoked by Susanna's nudity, as in Peter Riga's account, but simply by her face (48-49). Their lust can no longer be seen as the "natural" male response to unveiled female beauty; after all, many other men would have seen Susanna's face, and none of them tried

---

[25] Stevenson 2005b: 98. Some Church leaders did recognize the danger of false accusations for both nuns and married women. For example, Ambrose uses the story of Susanna's miraculous rescue by the intervention of God as part of his argument against imposing a gynecological exam on a consecrated virgin who had been anonymously accused of breaking her vows of celibacy (*Letter* 5). Similarly, Jerome references Susanna when telling the story of a Ligurian woman falsely accused of adultery, who miraculously survived her execution (*Letter* 1).
[26] The Vulgate is Jerome's late-fourth century Latin translation of the Bible. His translation of Daniel 13 is based on Theodotion's Greek version.

to proposition her. In this way, Willetrudis places the blame for the attempted violation squarely on the elders' corruption, not on Susanna's body.

Willetrudis frames their aggression through metaphors of violence: the elders are hunters laying traps (56-57), serpents waiting to strike (66); Susanna is the dove, lamb, or swan beset by wolves and kites (79-84, 91). Their advance is figured as a poisonous contamination, likened to the poisoning of Scylla by Circe from Ovid (67-70), imagery that heightens the sense of danger without focusing our attention on Susanna's physical appearance.[27] In this scene, Willetrudis breaks the frame of narration to address Susanna directly, prompting her audience to identify with Susanna's perspective rather than that of the aggressors (92-95). When Willetrudis does mention nudity, it is not to explain the elders' lust or linger on her physical charms, but simply to point out that she was physically defenseless against them—"when you were naked, trembling from fear among thieves" (95). Where Peter Riga's Susanna wavers, tossed like a boat between hope and fear (168-82), Willetrudis' Susanna is *immōbilis* (109): steady in virtue, though endangered in body.

Willetrudis' trial scene likewise reorients the focus. After being summoned, Susanna appears singing psalms, her devoutness

---

[27] Ovid, *Metamorphoses* 13.898-14.74. Peter Riga uses similar classical imagery to embellish his retelling of Susanna's story. Unlike Willetrudis though, he invokes the marine dangers posed by Charybdis and the Syrtes (which he uses almost as a synonym for Scylla) not to highlight the monstrosity of the elders' behavior, but to characterize Susanna's dilemma, caught between physical assault and the accusation of adultery (168-82; Mozley 1930: 31). See Dinkova-Bruun 2022 (esp. 423-27).

foregrounded (166). The elders command that she be stripped naked so they may gaze upon her *pudibunda* (173), the private parts her modesty typically keeps concealed, a detail Willetrudis again uses not to invite the reader's gaze but to underscore the elders' violence and perversion, for which Willetrudis wishes eternal damnation upon them (181). Here, the problem is unambiguously the elders' depravity, while Susanna is aligned with the virgin martyrs who endure violation and humiliation at the hands of corrupt judges. In a prayer to God, Susanna declares her unshakable trust in divine wisdom and embraces her ordeal as a martyrdom (215-221). When Daniel intervenes, Willetrudis narrates Daniel's inspired detective work, but soon brings Susanna back to the center of the poem. It is ultimately her virtue, not Daniel's brilliance, that secures her salvation.

By the conclusion, the entire community praises God and the virtue of Susanna, who is likened to Joseph, falsely accused of attempted rape by Potiphar's wife (333-336). The moral of Willetrudis' version is clear: Susanna's chastity, preserved against assault and false accusation, stands as a triumph of faith. Susanna—matron, martyr, victrix, and patroness—becomes a model not just of marital chastity, but, for Willetrudis' *sorōrēs,* of virginal fidelity to Christ the Bridegroom (344-368).

III. AUTHORSHIP & HISTORICAL CONTEXT

Willetrudis herself remains largely obscure. Her poem and attribution are preserved in a single extant manuscript, dating to

1240 and housed in the Bavarian State Library in Munich (Bayerische Staatsbibliothek, Clm 12513, fols. 23-35; Figure 7).[28]

The manuscript is an eclectic collection of medieval Latin poetry by a range of authors such as Hildebert of Lavardin and Bernard of Cluny. It was copied by a scribe named Liutold working in the Cistercian monastery of Raitenhaslach (roughly 70 miles from Munich), but that does not necessarily mean Willetrudis was connected to that monastery.[29] The quality of Willetrudis' Latin, her Classical references, and her subject matter all hint at a highly educated intellectual Christian woman. She was most likely a nun, possibly even an abbess.[30] In her prologue, she claims to use the model of Susanna as a means to fortify the morals of her *sorōrēs*, most likely her fellow nuns, and she repeatedly uses first-person plural verbs and feminine endings, suggestive of a community of female readers in particular. By the end of the poem, she exhorts Susanna to guide her *famulae* (344), handmaidens, a word regularly used for nuns in medieval Latin, and calls on "mothers, who have scorned love affairs" (354)—possibly referring to abbesses or senior nuns, the "mothers" of the convent—likewise to look to Susanna.

The name Willetrudis potentially points to a Frankish origin, and there was in fact a Willetrudis who was the first abbess of the Hohenvart Abbey in Bavaria in the late 11th century.

---

[28] The manuscript has been digitized and is available online at the Munich Digitalization Center

[29] Silagi (1999: 373) says it is nothing more than a tempting guess to associate Willetrudis with the Cistercian convent of Seligenthal in Landshut, which was founded in 1232 and under the pastoral care of Raitenhaslach beginning in 1426. See also https://arts.st-andrews.ac.uk/monasticmatrix/monasticon/seligenthal

[30] Stevenson 2005a: 130.

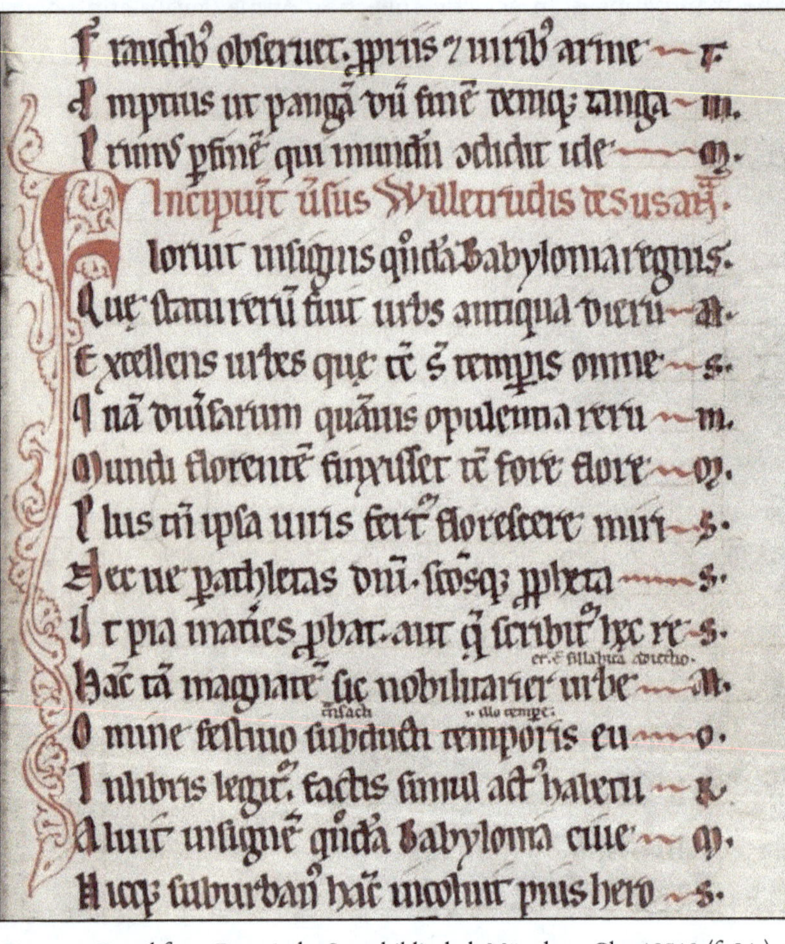

Figure 8: Detail from Bayerische Staatsbibliothek München, Clm 12513 (f. 24r). The rubricated letters read *Incipiunt versūs Willetrudis dē Sūsannā*.

The convent, however, does not seem to have been a literary center, and so Stevenson suggests we may instead identify our author as the "abbess Wiltrudis" (*sic*) named among the recent dead at Wilton Abbey in Wiltonshire, England in 1122.[31] Unlike at Hohenvart, the women of Wilton were especially known for their literary output. Among its most famous literary *alumnae* is Muriel of Wilton, who lived at the beginning of the 12th century. While none of her own poetry survives, she was considered an "illustrious poetess" (*inclyta versificātrīx*) whose grave was pointed out to pilgrims.[32] Male poets celebrated the work of Muriel, including Hildebert of Lavardin, whose work appears next to that of Willetrudis in our surviving manuscript. In a letter from Serlo, canon of Bayeux, who exchanged poems with Muriel, her community is admired as "a city rich in poetry" (*faecundam versibus urbem*, 3). In this same letter, Serlo anxiously thinks that her Vergil (*Marō vester,* 11) will ridicule his verse, acknowledging a classicizing literary culture at Wilton.[33] Such an environment suits the Willitrudis of *dē Sūsannā*, who freely quotes Vergil (prologue 11) and alludes to classical mythology (68ff, 328). The subject of Susanna itself might also have been particularly suited to Wilton, which, as a nunnery and convent school, served not just religious but also secular women, many of whom, like Susanna, would become wives.[34]

---

[31] Stevenson 2005a: 130.

[32] Herman of Laon and Tournai, *Dē mīrāculīs S. Mariae Laudunensis* 2.14 (PL 156, col. 983 A). See also Stevenson 2005b: 95.

[33] Both Surlo's and Hildebert's epistolary poems to Muriel can be most easily accessed online through Joan Ferrante's *Epistolae* project: https://epistolae.unisi.it/woman/26106.html

[34] Tyler (2017: 322-323) notes that Susanna also figures in other Wilton texts.

IV. THE LATIN OF *DĒ SŪSANNĀ*

The main body of the poem consists of 371 lines of verse, preceded by a 32 line prologue. The poem is composed in Leonine hexameter, a rhyming form of dactylic hexameter that was particularly popular in the Middle Ages. As in dactylic hexameter, each line consists of six feet, the first four of which can be either dactyls (– ∪ ∪) or spondees (– –). The fifth foot is usually a dactyl, and the sixth must be a spondee. In addition to the usual line-final anceps syllable, Leonine hexameter features an anceps syllable before each mid-line caesura. The final word of every line rhymes with the word before the caesura with varying degrees of fidelity (e.g., *suburbānus* / *hērōs*, 13; *tālis* / *quālis*, 23). Willetrudis often, although not invariably, uses parallel inflectional endings to create these rhymes (e.g., *sectandō* / *imitandō*, prologue 5).

The strict demands of Leonine hexameter and its rhyme scheme require Willetrudis to take numerous grammatical and lexical liberties in her composition. The manuscript features interlinear glosses offering *ad hoc* clarification on lines deemed to be especially unclear (see three examples near the bottom of Figure 8). These scribal glosses are provided in our commentary with translations. The poem itself features a very loose word order (e.g., 240-241), and postponed conjunctions and relative pronouns are used freely (e.g., *praecellit cīvēs, superēminet ac*, 16). In cases where the word order is especially unclear, we provide a suggested reordering in the comments. Subjunctives are substituted for expected indicatives twice, presumably to maintain the rhyme scheme (*observet*, prologue 30; *perdūcat*, 368). The vowel lengths necessary for correct scansion often deviate from standard usage. These deviations most consistently manifest in the shortening of final *-ē* in adverbs (e.g., *intime*, 147) and final *-ō*, particularly in first person singular verbs and ablative gerunds (e.g., *volo*, 75; *iūrando*, 184). The name *Sūsanna* frequently appears at the end of a line, resulting in a shortened *u* to accommodate the dactyl in the fifth foot. Several words undergo isolated changes in vowel length throughout, including *ōpiniōnis* for *opīniōnis* (15), *tibiīs* for *tībiīs* (307), and *mīrīfice* for *mīrificē* (323). All words in the text are macronized to allow for correct scansion, and all deviations from standard vowel length are noted in the comments. In addition to the meter, the Latin of *dē Sūsannā* features other characteristics of medieval Latin that may be unfamiliar to readers of Classical Latin. Notably, Willetrudis frequently employs the gerund in the ablative (*-ō*) in an expanded adverbial function, where Classical Latin might prefer a present participle or subordinate clause to express manner, means, cause, or attendant circumstances, a medieval Latin precursor to the present participle in Spanish and Italian.[35] Finally, like that of other medieval authors, Willetrudis' Latin frequently breaks the rules of the sequence of tenses (74, 132, 133).

Willetrudis' great facility with Latin is particularly evident in her creative word usage. Infinitives are frequently used substantively for cognate abstract nouns (e.g., *posse* for *potestātem*, 55 and 308; *velle* for *voluntātem*, 125). She also adapts existing Latin nouns to new declensional patterns as needed to fit the meter (e.g., *subsannā* for *subsannātiōne*, 21; *vītāmine* for *vītā*, 340), even substituting the

---

[35] Gerunds in the ablative used this way can also be found at prologue 5, prologue 8, 88, 95, 184, 208, 292, 322, 344, 357.

adjective *magnam* with the third declension noun *magnātem* in order to maintain the rhyme scheme (9). In line 29, she coins her own word: the otherwise unattested noun *coniectās, -tātis,* which seems to be derived from the verb *coniectō* with the abstract noun forming suffix *-tās, -tātis.* For metrical reasons, Willetrudis sometimes adds the archaic passive infinitive ending -er to classical passive infinitive endings (e.g., *nōbilitārier,* 9). The scribe comments on the occasional presence of this ending, explaining *er est sillabica adiectiō* ("the 'er' is a syllabic addition," see Figure 8, five lines from bottom). Her penchant for neologisms and archaisms, as well as her use of Greek loanwords (e.g., *dūlī/δοῦλοι,* 136), indicate that Willetrudis was likely influenced by the so-called "hermeneutic style" of Anglo-Latin literature.[36] In Willetrudis, we see an innovative poet who is equally comfortable working within and ranging beyond the Latin styles of her day.

V. ABOUT THIS EDITION: RATIONALE OF THE LATIN TEXT, VOCABULARY, AND COMMENTARY

This commentary is designed to make *dē Sūsannā* as accessible as possible to a range of Latin learners, whether or not they happen to be well versed in medieval Latin. For the most part, we retain the distinctively medieval features of the original orthography. The scribe frequently inserts *p* between nasals (e.g., *dampnis,* 304), and *c* and *t* are used interchangeably before *i* (e.g., *vicium,* 38), as are *y* and *i* in any position and *p* and *b* (e.g., *prespiteri,* 139 and *presbiteri,* 170). In such cases, we preserve the original medieval

---

[36] For more on the "hermeneutic style," see Lapidge 1975.

spelling in our text and in the on-page vocabulary, while also including the more familiar classical spelling in parentheses to help the reader more easily recognize the word. With the goal of accessibility in mind, we have made some small modifications to the original text. In the original manuscript, the scribe used an *e caudāta* (*ę*) or simply an unembellished *e* to represent the diphthong *ae*. For the sake of consistency and to make word forms more immediately recognizable to a classically trained audience, we transcribe both of these variants as *ae*. Exceptions are made only in instances where a short *e* was necessary for scansion (e.g., *premium*, 365).

The initial basis for the text of our edition was the transcription by Gabriel Silagi, with frequent consultation of the digitized copy of the original manuscript. Changes from both the manuscript and Silagi's edition have been made where necessary. We accept many of Silagi's textual emendations, namely the emendation of *rithmus* to *rithmīs* (prologue 27), *dactilicōs* to *dactilīs* (prologue 29), *maculātrīx* to *maculārum* (70), *concordas* to *concordāns* (150), *costāns* to *cōnstāns* (201), *fontem* to *sontem* (213), *invetante* to *inveterāte* (260), and *nūtum* to *mūtum* (321). We do, however, reject his emendation of *coniectātī* to *consectātī* (28).

We have also made several emendations of our own. We have emended *seu* to *ceu* (prologue 23) and *perclārum* to *praeclārum* (285). Many of our emendations are clustered in lines 85-86, a particularly puzzling sentence that appears to have been subject to scribal corruption (see Figure 11, p.57 below). In line 86, the manuscript contains the word *achles*, which is not firmly attested elsewhere. The one possible etymon, *achlis*, a Greek loan word referring to a "wild beast of the North," made little sense in context. This word can most readily be understood as an aberrant form of *athlēta*. In line 85, we have emended *foret* to *forēs* although this interpretation requires that the long *ē* be shortened to fit the meter (a poetic liberty that is not atypical of Willetrudis' verse). The sentence is addressed to Susanna, and good sense demands that she is the *memoranda patrōna* in question. Thus, a second person verb is most appropriate. Finally, Silagi transcribes the fifth word of line 85 as *sedis*. Upon closer examination of the original manuscript we read the word as *saeclīs*, written with a bare *e* in place of *ae* or *ę*. On two occasions, words in a line are repeated rather inexplicably, likely reflecting a scribal error (*est est*, 339; *istōs… istōs*, 253). In both instances, we have emended the redundant word to one that better fits the assumed meaning of the sentence and retained the rhyme scheme and meter (*est ast*; *istōs…ambōs*).

We have also added macrons to the text to aid scansion and to permit easier identification of grammatical forms. It should be noted that the vowel lengths needed for scansion occasionally differ from standard usage, sometimes in grammatically significant ways (e.g., *vīderis* for *vīderīs*, 266). In such instances, scansion takes precedence. Words have been macronized so that they scan correctly, and any deviations are noted in the comments.

The aim of our on-page vocabulary is to provide the words that an intermediate audience is least likely to know. Assuming that our audience is already well acquainted with the top 500 most frequently used Latin words (as per the Dickinson College Commentaries Latin Core Vocabulary List), we have excluded them from our on-page vocabulary, along with several other common words at our discretion. We provide a glossary at the end of the volume of all the words that are not defined on page. In order to avoid excessive repetition, words used four or more times are only defined the first time they are used. This frequently occurring vocabulary is provided below for easy reference.

The grammar in *dē Sūsannā* may be difficult for an audience at an intermediate reading level, especially one accustomed to Classical Latin, both because of the presence of grammatical features popularized in medieval Latin and because of Willetrudis' own innovation. The commentary seeks to address these complications, providing guidance in interpreting difficult lines and italicized glosses for especially opaque phrases, as well as literary, cultural, and historical context for Willetrudis' numerous intertextual allusions, biblical and otherwise.

BIBLIOGRAPHY

Bloch, R. Howard. 1991. *Medieval Misogyny and the Invention of Western Romantic Love*. Chicago University Press.

Brooks, Clive. 2007. *Reading Latin Poetry Aloud: A Practical Guide Guide to Two Thousand Years of Verse*. Cambridge University Press.

Churchill, Laurie J., Phyllis R. Brown, and Jane E. Jeffrey, eds. 2002. *Women Writing Latin: From Roman Antiquity to Early Modern Europe*. 3 vols. Routledge.

De Wet, Chris L. 2009. "The Reception of the *Susanna* Narrative (Dan. XIII; LXX) in Early Christianity." In *Septuagint and Reception*, edited by Johann Cook. Brill.

Dinkova-Bruun, Greti. 2022. "Scylla and Charybdis: Classical Marine Perils in Two Verse Bibles of the Later Middle Ages." In *'Omnium Magistra Virtutum': Studies in Honour of Danuta R. Shanzer*, edited by Andrew Cain and Gregory Hays. Brepols.

DiTommaso, Lorenzo. 2005. *The Book of Daniel and the Apocryphal Daniel Literature*. Brill.

Dronke, Peter. 1984. *Women Writers of the Middle Ages: A Critical Study of Texts from Perpetua to Marguerite Porete.* Cambridge University Press.

Jeffrey, David Lyle. 1996. "False Witness and the Just Use of Evidence in the Wycliffite *Pistel of Swete Susan.*" In *The Judgment of Susanna: Authority and Witness*, edited by Ellen Spolsky. Scholars Press.

Halpern-Amaru, Betsy. 1996. "The Journey of Susanna Among the Church Fathers." In *The Judgment of Susanna: Authority and Witness*, edited by Ellen Spolsky. Scholars Press.

Harrington, K. P., ed. *Medieval Latin.* 2nd ed. University of Chicago Press.

Lapidge, Michael. 1975. "The Hermeneutic Style in Tenth-Century Anglo-Latin Literature." *Anglo-Saxon England* 4: 67-111.

McAvoy, Liz Herbert. 2021. *The Enclosed Garden and the Medieval Religious Imaginary.* Boydell & Brewer.

Moore, Carey A., ed. 1977. *Daniel, Esther, and Jeremiah: The Additions.* Doubleday.

Mozley, J. H. 1930. "Susanna and the Elders: Three Medieval Poems." *Studi Medievali* 3: 27-52.

Natoli, Bartolo A., Angela Pitts, and Judith P. Hallett, eds. 2022. *Ancient Women Writers of Greece and Rome*. Routledge.

Silagi, Gabriel. 1999. "*Willetrudis Versus de Susanna*: Eine Unbeachtete Fraudendichtung Aus Dem 13. Jahrhundert." *Aevum* 73 (2): 371-384.

Smith, Kathryn A. 1993. "Inventing Marital Chastity: The Iconography of Susanna and the Elders in Early Christian Art." *Oxford Art Journal* 16 (1): 3-24.

Spolsky, Ellen, ed. 1996a. *The Judgment of Susanna: Authority and Witness*. Scholars Press.

—. 1996b. "Law or the Garden: The Betrayal of Susanna in Pastoral Painting." In *The Judgment of Susanna: Authority and Witness*, edited by Ellen Spolsky. Scholars Press.

Staley, Lynn. 2007. "Susanna and English Communities." *Traditio* 62: 25-58.

Stevenson, Jane. 2005a. *Women Latin Poets: Language, Gender, and Authority from Antiquity to the Eighteenth Century*. Oxford University Press.

—. 2005b. "Anglo-Latin Women Poets." In *Latin Learning and English Lore: Studies in Anglo-Saxon Literature for Michael Lapidge*, edited by Katherine O'Brien O'Keeffe and Andy Orchard. University of Toronto Press.

Thiébaux, Marcelle. 1994. *The Writings of Medieval Women: An Anthology*. Garland Publishing.

Tyler, Elizabeth Muir. 2017. *England in Europe: English Royal Women and Literary Patronage, c. 1000-1150*. University of Toronto Press.

Watt, Diane. 2020. *Women, Writing and Religion in England and Beyond, 650-1100*. Bloomsbury.

Wilpert, Giuseppe. 1903. *Roma sotterranea. Le pitture delle catacombs Romane, vol. 2, Tavole*. Desclée, Lefebvre, and C.

Ziolkowski, Jan M. 1996. "Towards a History of Medieval Latin Literature." In *Medieval Latin: An Introduction and Bibliographic Guide*, edited by F. A. C. Mantello and A. G. Rigg. The Catholic University of America Press.

FREQUENT VOCABULARY

Words that appear four (4) times or more in the text of *dē Sūsannā* are listed below, excluding general vocabulary, based on the DCC Latin Core Vocabulary List. Their full vocabulary entries are provided here and on the first page where they occur, but are otherwise omitted. We encourage students to memorize these words as soon as possible in order to facilitate their ease of reading this text.

āctus, -ūs m.: act, action; impulse

aevum, -ī n.: generation, age; eternity

agnus, -ī m.: lamb

almus, -a, -um: blesséd, kind

ambō, -ae, -ō: both

cernō, -ere, crēvī, certum: distinguish, discern, see; resolve, determine; decree

Chrīstus, -ī m.: Christ

cito (adv.): quickly

comitō (1): accompany, attend, follow

congrātulor (1): congratulate, rejoice, give thanks

cor, cordis n.: heart

creō (1): produce, beget, create

daemōn, -onis m.: spirit, demon

dampnō (CL: damnō) (1): find guilty, condemn

Daniēl (indeclinable): Daniel

dīves, -itis: rich, wealthy

dominus, -ī m.: master; the Lord

dōnec: while; until

ecce: lo! behold! look!

etenim: and indeed; for in fact

factum, -ī n.: deed

fors, fortis f.: chance, luck

Ioachim (indeclinable): Joachim, husband of Sūsanna

iūstus, -a, -um: just, righteous

lavō (1): wash, bathe

male: badly, wickedly; severely

medium, -iī n.: middle

meritum, -ī n.: a thing deserved, desert; service, reward, merit, value

nāta, -ae f.: daughter

ōstium (ML: hōstium), -iī n.: gate, door; entrance

pariter: likewise, at the same time; alike

pius, -a, -um: dutiful, loyal; sacred; merciful (when applied to God or Christ)

pōmērium (CL: pōmārium), -iī n.: garden

prāvus, -a, -um: crooked, perverse

prespiter (CL: presbyter), -erī m.: elder

prex, precis f.: prayer, request

probō (1): test, prove; approve, esteem; attest

reserō (1): open, reveal, expose

sānctus, -a, -um: venerable, holy

scīlicet (adv.): certainly, that is to say

senex, senis m.: elder

sēnsus, -ūs m.: perception, feeling; sense

sors, sortis f.: lot, fate

spērō (1): hope, believe, trust

spīritus, -ūs m.: breath, spirit; the Holy Spirit

Sūsanna, -ae f.: Susanna

tangō, -ere, tetigī, tāctum: touch, strike, reach; mention

ABBREVIATIONS

abl. ablative
acc. accusative
act. active
adj. adjective
adv. adverb
cf. compare to (*cōnfer*)
CL Classical Latin
dat. dative
e.g. for example
(*exemplī grātiā*)
fem. feminine
fut. future
gen. genitive
Grk. Greek
i.e. that is (*id est*)
imperf. imperfect

ind. indicative
inf. infinitive
lit. literally
masc. masculine
ML Medieval Latin
neut. neuter
nom. nominative
PL *Patrologia Latina*
pass. passive
perf. perfect
pl. plural
prep. preposition
pres. present
sg. singular
subj. subjunctive
voc. vocative

INCIPIT PROLOGUS WILLETRUDIS "DĒ SŪSANNĀ"

Cum sint cōnscrīpta iūstōrum circiter ācta

Ad laudem meritī, simul ad sōlāmina nostrī,

Quid proderit scītū, lēctor, sī forte cupītū

In loca rūmōris (nisi pāx hīs) nōn bene nōris

Ūtī sectandō, necnōn sectāns imitandō.   5

 āctum, -ī n.: deed

circiter: approximately

cōnscrībō, -ere, -scrīpsī,
 -scrīptum: write

imitor (1): imitate

iūstus, -a, -um: just, righteous

laus, laudis f.: praise, glory

lēctor, -ōris m.: reader

meritum, -ī n.: merit, service

necnōn: and also, and yet

prologus, -ī m.: prologue

prōsum, prōdesse, prōfuī,
 prōfutūrum: be of use, profit

rūmor, -ōris m.: rumor, fame

sector (1): follow

sōlāmen, -inis n.: comfort

---

cōnscrīpta: the final syllable falls in the anceps position before the caesura

Ad laudem: *ad* + an abstract noun here shows purpose

meritī, nostrī: objective gen.; *nostrī* is the pronoun ("of us"), not a possessive adj.

meritī: scribal gloss: *id est iūstōrum (that is, of the just)*

Quid…imitandō: *What benefit will there be in knowing [the deeds of the just], reader,
 [or] perhaps in desiring [to know] in place of rumor (except peace from these things
 [i.e., the enjoyment of reading]) if you do not rightly know how to make use of
 following [their example] and also, in following, of imitating..*

proderit = *prōderit*; W. treats the *o* as short for the meter

scītū, cupītū: supines from *sciō* and *cupiō*; abl. of specification with *proderit* (*what
 benefit will there be in knowing … [or] in desiring…*)

nōris = *nōveris*, fut. perf. indicative

Ūtī: object inf. dependent on *nōris*

sectandō, imitandō: abl. gerunds dependent on *Ūtī* (see section IV of the
 introduction for W.'s use of abl. gerunds)

Pertinget bravium certus sectātor eōrum.

Fortia facta Deī vel quem monet hōra diēī,

Illa tamen cūncta Chrīstī sub dogmate iūncta,

Ut reor, hīc nūllus sectandō complet homullus.

Hinc haec dicta putēs: "Nōn omnia possumus omnēs."　　10

---

bravīum, –ī n. (Grk. βραβεῖον):
 reward

Chrīstus, –ī m.: Christ

compleō, –ēre, –plēvī, –plētum:
 fill (up/in), complete, fulfill

dictum, –ī n.: word; saying

dogma, –atis n.: (religious)
 doctrine, teaching

factum, –ī n.: deed

homullus, –ī m.: little man,
 mortal

hōra, –ae f.: hour

iungō, –ere, iūnxī, iūnctum:
 join, unite

moneō, –ēre, –uī, –itum: warn;
 advise

pertingō, –ere, –tigī, –tāctum:
 attain

reor, rērī, ratus sum: think

sectātor, –ōris m.: follower

sector (1): follow

---

bravium = *bravīum*; W. treats the *i* as short for the meter

Fortia facta Deī: cf. Vergil *Aen.* 1.641 (*fortia facta patrum*)

quem: direct object of *monet*, whose subject is *facta … vel hōra*; the postponed
 antecedent is *homullus*

Illa: scribal gloss: *bona opera* (*good works*)

Illa … cūncta: acc. direct object of *complet*

hīc: *here on earth*

sectandō: abl. gerund used adverbially to show attendant circumstance (see
 section IV of the introduction for W.'s use of abl. gerunds)

putēs: jussive subj.

"Nōn omnia possumus omnēs": direct quotation from Vergil's *Eclogue* 8.63

Sed magis intentē satagit quī scandere mente

Culmina virtūtis, dabitur quīs summa salūtis,

Ūnice iūstōrum sequitur tunc quid studiōrum.

Fēcerat hoc Anna nātōs gignente Fenennā,

Innuba quae mānsit, dōnec Deus hanc magis auxit.   15

Anna, –ae f.: Hannah, the first wife of Elkanah

augeō, –ēre, auxī, auctum: increase, honor

culmen, –inis n.: top, height

Fenenna, –ae f.: Peninnah, the second wife of Elkanah

gignō, –ere, genuī, genitum: bear

innubus, –a, –um: unmarried, virgin

intentus, –a, –um: intent; expectant

salūs, –ūtis f.: safety, health; salvation

satagō, –ere, –tēgī, –tāctum: be busy with, strive for (+inf.)

scandō, –ere, –ī, –sum: climb, ascend

summa, –ae f.: summit, peak

Sūsanna, –ae f.: Susanna

ūnicē: especially, uniquely

---

satagit: the subject *quī* is postponed

quīs = *prō quibus* (*in return for which*); scribal gloss: *culminibus* (*for the heights*)

Ūnice = *Ūnicē*; W. treats the *e* as short for the meter

quid: scribal gloss: *id est aliquid* (*that is, anything*); direct object of *sequitur*

hoc: scans as *hocc*, making the *o* long by position

Anna: the short nom. ending falls in the anceps position before the caesura

Anna ... Fenennā: An allusion to 1 Samuel 1:2-2:21, which tells the story of Anna (or Hannah) and Fenenna (or Peninnah), the two wives of Elkanah. Fenenna provokes Anna with taunts about her inability to have children. Anna prays for a son, promising to dedicate him to God, and later gives birth to the prophet Samuel.

nātōs: direct object of *gignente*

Innuba: *childless*

Sīcque pudīciciā quondam studet alma Susanna,

Cum quā luctātur, dōnec magis inde probātur.

Hinc, monitae, mōrēs libeat mūnīre, sorōrēs,

Trāmite virtūtum, teneāmus nē male tūtum

Mentibus extīnctīs, subitō spōnsī venientis   20

Condignae dignīs sed ut inveniāmur in ymnīs,

---

almus, -a, -um: blessed, kind

condignus, -a, -um: wholly
 deserving (of) (+abl./gen.)

dōnec: while; until

**exstinguō, -ere, -stīnxī,
 -stīnctum**: extinguish, destroy

libet (libēre), -uit, -itum est: it is
 pleasing

luctor (1): struggle

male: badly

moneō, -ēre, -uī, -itum: warn;
 advise

mūniō, -īre, -īvī, -ītum: fortify

probō (1): test; approve, esteem

pudīcicia (CL: pudīcitia), -ae f.:
 chastity

quondam (adv.): formerly, once

spōnsus, -ī m.: bridegroom

studeō, -ēre, -uī: strive for

subitō (adv.): suddenly

trāmes, -itis m.: course, track

ymnus (CL: hymnus), -ī m.:
 song of praise, hymn

---

pudīciciā: abl. dependent on *studet* rather than expected dat.

studet, luctātur, probātur: historical presents

Susanna = *Sūsanna*; the name frequently appears at the end of a line with a short *u* to accommodate the meter

libeat: jussive subj.

teneāmus: subj. in a negative purpose clause with postponed *nē*

male tūtum: *unsafe* or *dangerous*

spōnsī: the term regularly alludes to Christ (cf. the Parable of the Ten Virgins in Matthew 25:1–13)

Condignae: predicate nom. dependent on *inveniāmur*; governs the gen. *spōnsī venientis*

Spōnsam cum spōnsus fovet altā nocte reversus.

Ad fōrmam iūstī ceu prō sōlāmine nostrī,

Ut speculī fōrmam spectēmus nōs: age normam.

Facta quidem magnae nōbīs imitanda Susannae,   25

Quae mānsit casta sub daemonis arte molestā.

---

castus, -a, -um: pure, chaste

ceu: as, as if

daemōn, -onis m.: spirit, demon

foveō, -ēre, fōvī, fōtum: warm, cherish

imitor (1): imitate

molestus, -a, -um: troublesome

norma, -ae f.: standard, rule

revertō, -ere, -ī, -sum: go back, return

sōlāmen, -inis n.: comfort, solace

speculum, -ī n.: mirror

spōnsa, -ae f.: betrothed, bride

spōnsus, -ī m.: bridegroom

---

iūstī: scribal gloss: *id est iūsticiae* [CL = *iūstitiae*] (*that is, of justice*)

ceu prō sōlāmine nostrī: *as if for our own comfort*

speculī: gen. with *fōrmam*; parallel to *fōrmam iūstī*

spectēmus: hortatory subj. with objects *Ad fōrmam iūstī* and *[ad] speculī fōrmam*: *let us look to the shape of justice … like to the shape of a mirror*

age normam: *uphold the standard*

nōbīs: dat. of agent dependent on *imitanda [sunt]*

imitanda: supply *sunt*

casta: the short nom. ending falls in the anceps position before the caesura

Dē quā perbellum rithmīs fōrmāre libellum
Complacuit mentī, modo sī placet altitonantī,
Quī mē dactilicīs rēptantem mōre soractis
Fraudibus observet. Propriīs et vīribus armet,   30
Prōmptius ut pangam, dum fīnem dēnique tangam
Prīmus per fīnem, quī mundum condidit īdem.

---

altitonāns, –antis: thundering
  from on high
armō (1): equip, arm
complaceō, –ēre, –uī, –itum: be
  very pleasing
condō, –ere, –didī, –ditum:
  found, make
dactylicus, –a, –um (Grk.
  δακτυλικός): dactylic
dēnique (adv.): finally, in the end
fōrmō (1): form, shape
fraus, fraudis f.: falsehood, error
libellus, –ī m.: little book

mundus, –ī m.: world
observō (1): watch, observe
pangō, –ere, pepigī, pactum: fix;
  agree upon; compose (poetry etc.)
perbellus, –a, –um: very pretty
prōmptus, –a, –um: ready, eager
proprius, –a, –um: one's own,
  special, characteristic
rēptō (1): crawl, creep
rithmus (CL: rhythmus), –ī m.:
  rhythm, verse
tangō, –ere, tetigī, tāctum:
  touch, reach; mention

---

altitonantī: i.e., God; an epithet used in CL for Jupiter
dactilicīs: modifies *fraudibus*: [*my*] *dactylic mistakes*
mōre soractis: *in the manner of a mouse* (i.e., timidly)
soractis: scribal gloss: *id est mūris* (*that is, of a mouse*); *soractis* appears to be an
  alternative gen. form of *sōrex, sōricis* m.: mouse, shrew
observet: subj. in place of expected ind. in order to rhyme with *armet*
Propriīs: adj. referring to God
Propriīs et vīribus: take *et* before *Propriīs*
armet: jussive subj. with implied *mē* as its direct object
tangam: subj. dependent on *dum*: *until I finally reach the end*

INCIPIUNT VERSŪS WILLETRUDIS "DĒ SŪSANNĀ"

Flōruit īnsignis quondam Babylōnia rēgnīs

Quae stātū rērum fuit urbs antīqua diērum,

Excellēns urbēs, quae tunc sunt temporis, omnēs,

Quam dīversārum quamvīs opulentia rērum

Mundī flōrentem finxisset tunc fore flōrem,   5

---

antīquus, -a, -um: old, ancient

Babylōnia, -ae f.: Babylonia, a kingdom between the Tigris and Euphrates *or* Babylon, its capital

dīversus, -a, -um: separate, various

excellō, -ere, -ui, -celsum: excel, surpass

fingō, -ere, fīnxī, fīctum: mold, shape; devise

flōreō, -ēre, -uī: blossom, flourish

flōs, flōris m.: flower, bloom

īnsignis, -e: eminent, famous

mundus, -ī m.: world, universe, heavens

opulentia, -ae f.: wealth, riches

quondam (adv.): formerly, once

status, -ūs m.: condition; status

versus, -ūs m.: line, verse

---

rēgnīs: *for its (royal) power*; abl. of cause dependent on *īnsignis*

stātū = *statū*; W. treats the *a* as long for the meter

stātū rērum: *in the status of things* (i.e., by the standard of the time)

fuit urbs antīqua: cf. Vergil *Aen.* 1.12 (*urbs antīqua fuit*)

tunc … temporis: *existed at that time*

Quam: relative pronoun with *urbs* as its antecedent; subject of *fore* in an acc. + inf. construction introduced by *finxisset*

dīversārum … rērum: *wealth of various riches*

finxisset: pluperf. subj. in a concessive clause introduced by *quamvīs*

fore: fut. inf. of *sum*, dependent on *finxisset*: *had shaped to be*

Plūs tamen ipsa virīs fertur flōrēscere mīrīs,

Necne per āthlētās Dominī sānctōsque prophētās,

Ut pia māteriēs probat aut, quae scrībitur, haec rēs.

Hanc tam magnātem sīc nōbilitārier urbem

Ōmine fēstīvō subductī temporis aevō   10

In librīs legitur, factīs simul āctus habētur.

āctus, -ūs m.: act, action; impulse

aevum, -ī n.: generation, age;
 eternity

dominus, -ī m.: master, the Lord

fēstīvus, -a, -um: agreeable,
 joyous

flōrēscō, -ere, —, —: blossom,
 flower

liber, librī m.: book

māteriēs, -ēī f.: subject matter

mīrus, -a, -um: marvelous

nōbilitō (1): ennoble

ōmen, -inis n.: omen, token

plūs (adv.): more; furthermore

prophēta, -ae m.: prophet

quondam (adv.): formerly, once

sānctus, -a, -um: venerable, holy

subdūcō, -ere, -duxī, -ductum:
 draw up, raise; take away

---

fertur: *is said,* introduces indirect statement with *flōrēscere*

Necne = *necnōn* (*and also*)

āthlētās Dominī: *champions of the Lord* (i.e., martyrs)

pia māteriēs: i.e., the religious tradition

haec rēs: i.e., Susanna's story

magnātem = *magnam*

nōbilitārier: *-ier* is an archaic pass. inf. ending; scribal gloss: *er est sillabica adiectio*
 (*the "er" is a syllabic addition*); inf. in indirect statement introduced by *legitur*

urbem: subject acc. in an indirect statement introduced by *legitur*

subductī … aevō: *in the age of a time now passed*

subductī: scribal gloss: *trānsāctī* (*completed, bygone*)

temporis: scribal gloss: *id est illō tempore* (*that is, at that time*)

habētur: *it is considered* [*to be*]

Aluit īnsignem quondam Babylōnia cīvem,
Hicque suburbānus hanc incoluit pius hērōs
Nōbilitāns urbem, bene quam diffāmat in orbem,
Fāma suī digna, causa ōpiniōnis, et alma   15
Praecellit cīvēs, superēminet ac quia dīves.

---

alō, -ere, -uī, altum: nourish, rear
diffāmō (1): spread news of, make
  widely known
dīves, -itis: rich, wealthy
hērōs, -ōis m. (Grk. ἥρως): hero
incolō, -ere, -uī: inhabit
nōbilitō (1): ennoble
opīniō, -ōnis f.: opinion; rumor;
  reputation

pius, -a, -um: dutiful, loyal; sacred
praecellō, -ere, —, —: surpass,
  excel
suburbānus, -a, -um: near the
  city
superēmineō, -ēre, —, —: rise
  above

---

suburbānus: the final syllable falls in the anceps position before the caesura
Fāma...alma: *his worthy and kind reputation, the cause of his esteem; fāma* is the
nom. subject of *praecellit*. Alternatively, it may be abl. with Joachim as the implied
subject of *praecellit*: *he surpasses all citizens with his worthy and kind reputation*. In
this case, *suī* would scan as one syllable.
digna: the short nom. (or long abl.) ending falls in the anceps position before the
caesura
ōpiniōnis = *opīniōnis*; W. treats the first *o* as long and the first *i* as short for the
meter
superēminet ac = *ac superēminet*; subject is Joachim
quia dīves: supply *est*

Quī vir sublīmis ad dignaque quaeque reclīnis
Est Ioachim dictus, summā dē stirpe creātus.
Hic sibi mērito prīmōrēs cōnscīvit honōrēs,
Inter concīvēs faciēns bona prōmptior omnēs.   20
Huic sine subsannā nūpsit tunc pulchra Susanna,
Prōgenita Helchīā, nātō dē germine Iūda.

---

concīvis, –is m.: fellow-citizen

cōnsciscō, –ere, –vīi/–iīi, –īitum:
 approve of, bring upon oneself

creō (1): produce, beget

germen, –inis n.: seed, bloodline

Helchīa, –ae. m.: Helchia, father
 of Susanna

honōs, –ōris m.: esteem, honor

Ioachim (indeclinable): Joachim,
 husband of Susanna

Iūda (indeclinable): Judah

meritō (adv.): deservedly

nūbō, –ere, nūpsī, nūptum: (of a
 bride) be married to (+dat.);
 marry

prīmōris, –e: first; foremost

prōgignō, –ere, –genuī,
 –genitum: beget

prōmptus, –a, –um: eager, quick,
 ready

reclīnis, –e: leaning back, inclined

stirps, stirpis f.: family tree, stock

sublīmis, –e: lofty, noble

---

sublīmis: the final syllable falls in the anceps position before the caesura

sublīmis, reclīnis: the two adjectives are joined by the *-que* in *dignaque*

Ioachim: take as predicate nom.

mērito = *meritō*; W. treats the *e* as long and the *o* as short for the meter

sine subsannā = *sine subsannātiōne (without derision)*; a pun on Susanna's name

Susanna = *Sūsanna*; see note on line 16 of the prologue

Helchīā: abl. of source

nātō: modifies *Helchīā*

Iūda: take as gen. modifying *germine*

Virgō etenim tālis, cui nōn foret altera quālis,

Fīxerat haec mentī: semper servīre tonantī,

Nātam māterna docet ut vel cūra paterna.   25

Nam fuerant iūstī servantēs iussa Moȳsī,

Fīlia pollentēs similat quōs alma parentēs.

---

etenim: and indeed; for in fact

fīgō, -ere, fīxī, fīxum: fix, fasten

iussum, -ī n.: command, order

māternus, -a, -um: maternal

Moȳses, -ī m.: Moses

nāta, -ae f.: daughter

paternus, -a, -um: paternal

polleō, -ēre, —, —: be strong, be
esteemed, prevail in (+abl.)

serviō, -īre, -īvī, -ītum (+dat.):
serve

servō (1): preserve, observe

similō (1): imitate, resemble

Sūsanna, -ae f.: Susanna

tonō, -āre, -uī: thunder

---

cui ... quālis: *to whom no other might compare.* The dat. *cui* parallels the common
construction of the dat. with adjectives of likeness (e.g., *similis*).

foret = *esset*; imperf. subj. in a relative clause of characteristic

mentī: i-stem abl. form used in place of *mente* to maintain the rhyme scheme; abl.
of place where

tonantī: *the thundering one*; see note on *altitonantī* in line 28 of the prologue

Nātam ... paterna: *just as maternal and paternal care instructs a daughter [to do]*

māterna: the short nom. ending falls in the anceps position before the caesura

ut: *ut (just as)* has been postponed to the middle of the line

vel: in ML, *vel* can mean "and" as well as "or." Here, it is best translated as "and."

Fīlia ... parentēs: rearrange: *pollentēs parentēs quōs fīlia alma similat*

Hāc coniectātī fēlīx ac coniuge tālī

Inclitus hic Ioachim pollēbat honōre virītim,

Quandoquidem dīves fuit atque benignus in omnēs.   30

Huius pōmerium domuī fuit ecce propinquum,

Ad quem Iūdaeī veniunt simul ac Pharisaeī

Quod sit honōrātus prae cūnctīs atque probātus.

---

coniectās, -tātis f.: union

coniūnx, -iugis f.: spouse, wife

benignus, -a, -um: kind,
 generous

ecce: lo! behold! look!

honōrō (1): honor, dignify

honōs, -ōris m.: esteem, honor

inclitus (inclutus), -a, -um:
 famous, glorious, renowned

Iūdaeus, -a, -um: of Judaea,
 Jewish

**Pharisaeus, -ī m. (Grk.
 Φαρισαῖος)**: Pharisee, a member
 of an ancient Jewish sect

polleō, -ēre, —, —: be strong, be
 esteemed, prevail in (+abl.)

**pōmerium (CL: pōmārium), -iī
 n.**: orchard

prae (+abl.): before

propinquus, -a, -um (+dat.):
 near, neighboring

quandoquidem: because

virītim (adj.): individually

Hāc coniectātī: *with this union*; W. appears to have created an otherwise
 unattested noun, *coniectās, -tātis* f., derived from the verb *coniectō* with the abstract
 noun forming suffix *-tās, -tātis*. Like with *mentī* (line 24), it is an i-stem abl. to
 maintain the rhyme.

virītim: *each man*

Ad quem: scribal gloss: *scīlicet Ioachim* (*namely Joachim*)

sit: subj. in a causal clause

Hīc solitī iūra semper renovāre paterna
Intereā sēnēs—āh sānē mentis inānēs—   35
Plēbem rēctūrī signantur in ōrdine bīnī,
Dē quibus omnipotēns monet istaec nōs, ita dīcēns:

---

bīnī, -ae, -a: two by two, two

inānis, -e: empty, worthless;
  devoid (of) (+gen.)

intereā (adv.): meanwhile, (ML) at
  this time

istic, istaec, istoc: this very

moneō, -ēre, -uī, -itum: warn;
  advise

omnipotēns, -entis: all-powerful,
  almighty

paternus, -a, -um: paternal

plēbs, plēbis f.: common people

renovō (1): restore, renew

sānē: truly, really

signō (1): designate, signify, mark

soleō, -ēre, solitus sum: be
  accustomed

---

solitī: agrees with *senēs* (the postponed subject of the sentence); sets up the
  complementary inf. *renovāre*, which takes the direct object *iūra ... paterna*

iūra: the short acc. ending falls in the anceps position before the caesura

intereā: cf. Daniel 13:5: *in illō annō (in that year)*, evidently referring to the year
  that Susanna and Joachim married

sēnēs = *senēs*; W. treats the first *e* as long for the meter

rēctūrī: fut. active participle expressing purpose with *signantur*

signantur in ōrdine bīnī: *are designated in pairs* (i.e., two judges are chosen)

monet ... nōs: *warns us [about] these [following] things*

Dē quibus ... docendus: cf. Daniel 13:5: *... dē quibus locūtus est Dominus: Quia
  ēgressa est inīquitās dē Babylōne ā seniōribus iūdicibus, quī vidēbantur regere populum;*
  possibly a reference to Jeremiah 29:20-23, which describes the punishment of the
  adulterous prophets Ahab and Zedekiah

Ēgreditur vērē vicium Babylōnis ab urbe
Dē senibusque virīs iūs quīs est condere iūris
Quīsque regī populus dēbēbat rīte docendus.   40
Hīque frequentābant Ioachim, velut ante solēbant,
Ad quōs conveniunt cūnctī, quīs iūra dedērunt,
Et domus haec Ioachim populō dat iūra diātim.

Babylōn, –ōnis f.: Babylon, the
  ancient and renowned chief city
  of Babylonia
condō, –ere, –didī, –ditum: lay
  down, build, found
conveniō, –īre, –vēnī, –ventum:
  meet, assemble
diātim (adv.): daily, every day
ēgredior, –ī, ēgressus sum: stride
  out, depart, disembark
frequentō (1): crowd together,
  frequent, visit

regō, –ere, rēxī, rēctum: rule,
  guide
rīte: in a proper manner, rightly,
  with correct religious procedure
senex, senis m.: elder
soleō, –ēre, solitus sum: be
  accustomed
vicium (CL: vitium), –iī n.:
  blemish, fault, sin
vērē: truly

---

iūs quīs est condere iūris: *for whom it is lawful to lay down the law*
quīs = *quibus*
Quīsque: scribal gloss: *prō quibus* (*by whom*); in ML, *prō* + abl. can be equivalent to
  per + acc., here to show agency; the *-que* is the enclitic "and"
rīte: can be taken either with the participle *docendus* or the pass. inf. *regī*, or with
  both
Hīque: i.e., the elders
quīs = *quibus*; relative pronoun with *cūnctī* as its antecedent
Ioachim: take as possessive gen. with *domus*, the subject of *dat*

Cumque revertisset populus, quī iūra petīsset,

Sūsannae mōris hoc certīs mānsit in hōrīs: 45

Intrat pōmerium, domuī quod forte propinquum

Imminet, ac fontis placidīs sē balneat undīs.

Dumque senēs pulchram sedulō vīdēre Susannam

Perfūsam faciē croceō vernāre colōre,

---

balneor (1): bathe

croceus, -a, -um: saffron-colored

hōra, -ae f.: hour

immineō, -ēre, —, — (+dat): overhang, border upon

intrō (1): enter

placidus, -a, -um: agreeable, pleasant

propinquus, -a, -um: near, neighboring

revertō, -ere, -ī, -sum: turn back, go back, return

sēdulō (adv.): eagerly

vernō (1): appear like spring, bloom

---

revertisset: pluperf. subj. in a circumstantial *cum* clause. The meaning here is not that the people return to Joachim's house but that they depart for a midday break (cf. Daniel 13:7: *Cum autem populus revertisset per merīdiem ... [And when the people departed at midday ...]*). This distinction is even clearer in Theodotion's ancient Greek version (καὶ ἐγένετο ἡνίκα ἀπέτρεχεν [= departed] ὁ λαὸς μέσον ἡμέρας ... [*And it happened when the people departed at midday ...*]).

petīsset = *petīvisset*; pluperf. subj. in a relative clause of characteristic

Sūsannae ... mānsit: *this remained the custom of Susanna*

mōris: the final syllable falls in the anceps position before the caesura

domuī: dat. dependent on *Imminet*; can also be taken with *propinquum*

sedulō = *sēdulō*; W. treats the *e* as short for the meter

Susannam = *Sūsannam*; see note on line 16 of the prologue

Perfūsam ... colōre: *imbued in her face with golden color*

vernāre: inf. in an indirect statement introduced by *vīdēre* with *Susannam* as subject acc.

Incidit in mentem coniungier hanc renitentem   50
Sordibus illicitīs sibi, lēgibus atque solūtīs.
Cor subvertēbant, nec caelum mente vidēbant,
Ipsīusque Deī minimum iuvat hōs reminīscī.
Dēnique sēductī sunt effectum sibi pactī,
Cum prīmum nactī sunt posse huius malefactī.   55

---

coniungō, -ere, -iūnxi, -iūnctum: join together, unite

cor, cordis n.: heart

dēnique (adv.): finally, in the end

effectus, -ūs, m.: fulfillment, accomplishment

illicitus, -a, -um: not allowed, unlawful, illicit

incidō, -ere, -ī: fall upon, fall into

malefactum, -ī n.: evil deed

minimus, -a, -um: least, smallest

nancīscor, -ī, nactus sum: obtain, find, stumble on

pacīscor, -ī, pactus sum: agree (on)

reminīscor, -ī (+gen.): call to mind; recall

reniteō, -ēre, —, —: shine back, flash

sēdūcō, -ere, -dūxī, -ductum: lead apart or away

solūtus, -a, -um: unbound, free

sordēs, -is f.: filth

subvertō, -ere, -ī, -sum: destroy, subvert

Incidit in mentem: *it occurred* [*to them*]

coniungier: pass. inf. subject of *incidit* with *hanc* as subject acc.

renitentem: scribal gloss: *id est fulgentem* (*that is, shining*)

sibi: take with *coniungier*

lēgibus atque = *atque lēgibus*

reminīscī: pres. inf. functioning as the subject of *iuvat*

effectum: acc. direct object of *pactī*

posse = *potestātem* (acc. sg. of *potestās*, here: *ability, opportunity*)

posse … malefactī: *the opportunity for this evil deed*; *malefactī* is an objective gen.

Īnsidiās tendunt sē pōmerīōque recondunt,

Ac velutī sollers quam prēndit turturis auceps,

Angulī in obscūrō—quis crēdere possit hoc?—ergō

Cum vērō domna vernantī fronte Susanna,

---

angulus, -ī m.: corner, nook,
 lurking-place

auceps, -cupis m.: fowler,
 someone who hunts birds

frōns, frōntis f.: forehead, brow

īnsidiae, -ārum f. pl.: ambush,
 plot

obscūrus, -a, -um: dim, dark

**prēndō (prehendō), -ere, -ī,
 -sum (+gen./acc.):** snatch, seize

recondō, -ere, -didī, -ditum:
 hide

sollers, -ertis: skilled, expert

tendō, -ere, tetendī, tentum:
 stretch, extend, set out

turtur, -uris m.: turtle-dove

vernō (1): flourish, appear
 springlike

---

sē: reflexive dependent on *recondunt*, not *tendunt*

velutī ... quam: *just as skilled as*

turturis: gen. object of *prēndit*

Angulī in obscūrō: *in the dark of a corner; obscūrō is used as a substantive here*

possit: potential subj.

Cum ... Intrat: the verb of the *cum* clause is postponed to line 64; the object
 (*Pōmerium*) is in line 62

domna: syncopated form of *domina*; the short nom. ending falls in the anceps
 position before the caesura

vernantī fronte: abl. of description

Susanna = *Sūsanna*; see note on line 16 of the prologue

Līlia flōrēscēns, roseō fulgōre rubēscēns,   60
(Ut fuerat suēta) famulābus tunc comitāta
Pōmeriumque virī—voluit quia fonte lavārī,
Nam fervēns aestus fuerat tum valde molestus,
Intrat sēcūra—quaenam sit huic ibi cūra?

---

aestus, -ūs m.: heat
comitō (1): accompany, attend, follow
famula, -ae f.: female house slave, handmaiden
ferveō, -ēre, fervī: blaze, boil
flōrēscō, -ere, —, —: blossom, flower, bloom
fulgor, -ōris m.: brightness
intrō (1): enter
lavō (1): wash, bathe
līlium, -iī n.: lily

molestus, -a, -um: troublesome, annoying
quisnam (quīnam), quaenam, quidnam: who indeed? what indeed?
roseus, -a, -um: rosy
rubēscō, -ere, -rubuī: begin to glow, redden
sēcūrus, -a, -um: calm, unworried
suēscō, -ere, suēvī, suētum: become accustomed, used, accustomed
valdē: greatly, very, intensely

Līlia: feminized form of *līlium, -ī n.* in apposition to Susanna. The name Susanna is derived from the Hebrew word for lily (*shoshan* or *Shoshannah*).

suēta: scans as two syllables with *su* treated as one consonant (cf. *qu* and *gu*); the short nom. ending falls in the anceps position before the caesura

famulābus: alternate form of *famulīs* to clarify fem. gender

valde = *valdē*; W. treats the *e* as short for the meter

sēcūra: the short nom. ending falls in the anceps position before the caesura

sit: potential subj.

huic: dat. of reference

Nōn erat hīc quisquam seniōrēs praeter et ipsam,   65

Āstū serpentēs nec sentit fonte latentēs,

Dē quōrum saevīs erat īnficienda venēnīs,

Ut dūdum Scylla, quam nārrat fābula Graeca,

---

astus, –ūs m.: cunning

dūdum (adv.): formerly

fābula, –ae f.: story, tale, fable

Graecus, –a, –um: Greek

īnficiō, –ere, –fēcī, –fectum:
taint, infect; poison; stain

lateō, –ēre, –uī: lie hidden, be
hidden

nārrō (1): narrate, tell, describe

praeter (+acc.): except

Scylla, –ae f.: Scylla, a
sea-monster

serpēns, –entis m./f.: snake,
serpent

venēnum, –ī n.: poison

---

praeter: prep. goes with both *seniōrēs* and *ipsam*

Āstū: abl. of manner with *latentēs*

Dē … venēnīs: rearrange: *dē saevīs venēnīs quōrum erat īnficienda*; scribal gloss:
Nota fābulās ("Note the myths," see Figure 9 below)

Scylla: According to Ovid (*Metamorphoses* 13.898-14.74), after Scylla rejected the
sexual advances of Glaucus, he sought aid from Circe, who poisoned the water
where Scylla bathed, causing her to transform into a monstrous sea-creature with
multiple dog-like heads around her waist. The short nom. ending falls in the
anceps position before the caesura

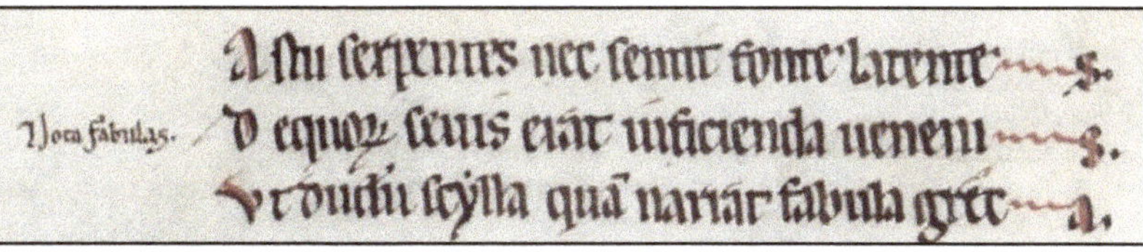

Figure 9. Detail from Bayerische Staatsbibliothek München, Clm 12513 (f. 25v).
The scribal comment *Nota fabulās* appears at left.

Invidiam Cyrcae saevae quasi passa novercae,

Cum gerit in pelle maculārum mīlia mīlle.   70

Quae tum causa virīs, aut quae mēns extat amōris,

Cum sōlī sōlam vīdissent fonte lavandam?

Namque lavanda duās, quibus est comitāta, puellās

Smīgmata quō ferrent, iubet hinc ut prōtinus īrent.

Cyrcē (CL: Circē), –ae f.: Circe, a sorceress

ex(s)tō (1): stand out; rise above

invidia, –ae f.: envy, jealousy

macula, –ae f.: spot; stain; blemish

mīlia, –ium n. pl.: thousands

noverca, –ae f.: stepmother

pellis, pellis f.: skin, hide

prōtinus (adv.): immediately, at once

quasi: as if, just as if, as though

smīgma, –ătis n. (Grk. σμῆγμα): cleansing soap, ointment

Invidiam: acc. direct object of *passa*, from *patior, –ī, passus sum*

quasi … novercae: *just like that* (i.e., *the envy*) *of a stepmother*; the envious stepmother is a common trope in classical literature

pelle: the final syllable falls in the anceps position before the caesura

maculārum mīlia mīlle: lit., *a thousand thousands of blemishes*

Quae, quae: interrogative adjectives agreeing with *causa* and *mēns*

mēns … amōris: *intent for passion*; *amōris* is an objective gen.

lavandam, lavanda: *about to wash*; in ML, gerundives tend to denote more futurity than obligation

iubet: governs both an indirect question (*quō ferrent*) and an indirect command (*ut…īrent*)

"Ōstia pōmeriī," dīcēns, "volo fonte lavārī,   75

Claudite post dorsum, necnōn properāte reversum."

Quae mox ēgressae complent, quod sunt ibi iussae.

Quam simplex fraudis fuerās simul īnscia sortis,

Digna columba patris, pateris quae tālia fraudis.

---

columba, -ae f.: pigeon, dove

compleō, -ēre, -plēvī, -plētum: finish, complete

dorsum, -ī n.: the back

ēgredior, -ī, ēgressus sum: depart

fraus, fraudis f.: fraud; trickery, deceit

īnscius, -a, -um: unaware, ignorant

necnōn: and also, and yet

ōstium (ML: hōstium), -iī n.: door; entrance

properō (1): hasten, speed

revertor, -ī, reversus sum: return

simplex, -icis: naïve

sors, sortis f.: lot, fate

Ōstia pōmeriī: object of *claudite*

volo = *volō*; W. treats the final *o* as short for the meter

properāte reversum: *hasten to return*; *reversum* is an acc. supine expressing purpose after a verb of motion

Quae: *and they* (i.e., *puellae*); connective relative

quod ... iussae: [*id*] *quod sunt ibi iussae* [*facere*]

Quam ... sortis: *How naive to deceit and how unaware of* [*your*] *fate you had been*

quae: take *columba* as antecedent; *pateris* (from *patior*) is the verb of the relative clause

Ac velutī cygnus—vel quod magis est: tener agnus!— 80

Ac velutī cygnus, sequitur quem prēndere mīlvus,

Raptat quemve lupus subitō occurrēns tener agnus,

Ōre tenēre lupī rōstrōve tenēbere mīlvī,

Sed tū forte lupō simul ac raptābere mīlvō,

---

agnus, –ī m.: lamb

cygnus (CL: cycnus), –ī m.: swan

fors, fortis f.: chance, luck

lupus, –ī m.: wolf

mīlvus, –ī m.: bird of prey, kite

occurrō, –ere, –ī, –sum (+dat):
 run to meet

prēndō (prehendō), –ere, –ī,
 –sum (+gen./acc.): snatch, seize

raptō (1): seize violently

rōstrum, –ī n.: beak

subitō (adv.): suddenly,
 unexpectedly

Ac velutī: *and just like*; introduces an extended simile from lines 80–84

vel quod magis est: *or what is better*; by comparing Susanna to a lamb, W. is
 portraying her as a Christ-like figure

prēndere: inf. indicating purpose with a verb of motion

quemve: take *agnus* as antecedent; *raptat* is the verb of the relative clause

tenēre = *tenēris,* 2nd person sg., pres. pass.

tenēbere, raptābere = *tenēberis, raptāberis,* 2nd person sg., fut. pass.

Figure 10. Susanna as a lamb and the elders as sheep,
fresco from the Catacombs of Praetextatus, Rome, fourth century CE.
Wilpert 1903, tav. 251.

Dum fores hīc sōla saeclīs memoranda patrōna   85
Athlēta. Ecce senēs, sua quōs prōtervia inānēs

āthlēta, -ae m.: champion
inānis, -e: empty; vain, foolish
memorō (1) (+gen./acc.):
  remember
patrōna, -ae f.: protectress,
  patroness

protervitās, -ātis f.: impudence
saeclum (saeculum), -ī n.:
  generation; age

---

fores = *forēs* = *essēs*, imperf. subj.; W. treats the *e* as short for the meter
sōla: the short nom. ending falls in the anceps position before the caesura
saeclīs memoranda: *to be remembered for the ages*
Athlēta: *Champion [of the Lord]*; in apposition to *patrōna*; this *Athlēta* is our
  emendation for the manuscript reading of *Achles* (see Figure 11 below and p. 26
  above)
prōtervia = *protervia*; W. treats the *o* as long for the meter

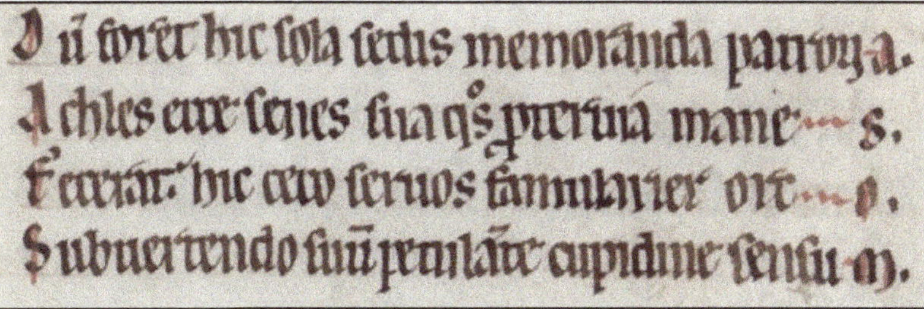

Figure 11. Detail of lines 85-88.
Bayerische Staatsbibliothek München, Clm 12513 (f. 25v).

Fēcerat hīc caecō servōs famulārier Orcō,

Subvertendo suum petulante cupīdine sēnsum,

Invāsēre piam, cupiunt quam valdē, Susannam

Vallō pōmeriī, quō sē voluēre recondī,   90

Ut solet ipse lupus, cui forte occurrerit agnus.

Quis fuerat sēnsus vel quālis erat tuus āctus,

Ō veneranda Deī, cernēns hīs tē male tangī?

---

caecus, -a, -um: blind

cernō, -ere, crēvī, certum:
  distinguish, discern, see

cupīdō, -inis f.: desire, eagerness

famulor (1) (+dat.): be a servant

invādō, -ere, -vāsī, -vāsum: go
  in, attack, invade

occurrō, -ere, -ī, -sum (+dat.):
  run to meet

Orcus, -ī m.: the lower world;
  hell; god of the underworld

petulāns, -antis: impudent

recondō, -ere, -didī, -ditum:
  hide, conceal, bury

sēnsus, -ūs m.: feeling; reason

subvertō, -ere, -ī, -sum: overturn;
  overthrow, destroy, subvert

valdē: strongly

vallum, -ī n.: fortification, wall

venerandus, -a, -um: revered,
  venerable

---

hīc: i.e., *here on Earth*

famulārier = *famulāri*; object inf. of *fēcerat* with *inānēs servōs* as the subject acc.

Subvertendo: abl. gerund used adverbially to express cause, means, or attendant
  circumstances (see section IV of the introduction for W.'s use of abl. gerunds);
  W. treats the *o* as short for the meter

Invāsēre = *Invāsērunt*

Susannam = *Sūsannam*; see note on line 16 of the prologue

Vallō = *in vallō*

quō … recondī: *where they wished to be hidden*

voluēre = *voluērunt*

Quis: = *quī* (interrogative adjective with *sēnsus*)

Quōs dēs aut gemitūs, aut quālēs corpore gestūs,

Cum nūdāta forēs inter pavitandō latrōnēs?   95

At tua mēns Dominō riguit cōnfīsa benignō,

In sē spērantēs quī dat cito congratulantēs,

---

benignus, -a, -um: kind, generous

cito (adv.): quickly

cōnfīdō, -ere, cōnfīsus sum (+dat.): have confidence in, be assured of

congrātulor (1): congratulate, rejoice, give thanks

gemitus, -ūs m.: groan

gestus, -ūs m.: motion, gesture

latrō, -ōnis m.: robber, thief

nūdō (1): bare, uncover, strip

pavitō (1): tremble, quake with fear; be terrified

rigēscō, -ere, riguī: stiffen, harden

soleō, -ēre, solitus sum: be accustomed

spērō (1): hope, believe, trust

---

dēs: subj. in a deliberative question

forēs = *essēs*; imperf. subj. in a circumstantial *cum* clause

pavitandō: abl. gerund used adverbially to express attendant circumstance (see section IV of the introduction for W.'s use of abl. gerunds); W. treats the *o* as short for the meter

In … congratulantēs: *Who swiftly makes those trusting in Him thankful*; c.f. Daniel 13:60: *quī salvat spērantēs in sē*

congratulantēs = *congrātulantēs*; W. treats the first *a* as short for the meter

Dēprōmuntque suum cōnspīrantēs male vōtum,

Vōceque cum tālī persuādent fornier illī:

"Cēde voluntātī, tibi quō maneāmus amātī.   100

Omnia sunt tūta: sunt hōstia nempe serāta.

Iam nē tardēris, sed enim per pignus amōris

Commiscēre volēns nōbīscum. Sī quoque nōlēns

Nōs dētestēris, modo post haec tū lapidēris."

---

commisceō, -ēre, -uī, -mixtum:
  mix together; blend, mingle
cōnspīrō (1): sound together;
  conspire
dēprōmō, -ere, -prōmpsī,
  -prōmptum: draw forth, utter
dētestor (1): denounce; ward off
fornicor (1): fornicate
hōstium (CL: ōstium), -iī n.:
  gate, door

lapidō (1): stone
nempe (adv.): indeed, to be sure,
  truly
persuādeō, -ēre, -suāsī, -suāsum
  (+dat.): persuade, convince
pīgnus, -oris n.: pledge, stake
sērō (1): fasten with a bolt, bar
tardō (1): loiter, delay
voluntās, -ātis f.: will, desire;
  purpose

---

cōnspīrantēs: substantive participle: *the conspirators*

persuādent: *they attempt to persuade*; conative pres.

fornier = *fornicārier* = *fornicārī*, pass. inf.

voluntātī: dat. dependent on *cēde*

quō maneāmus = *ut maneāmus*, purpose clause

tūta: the short nom. ending falls in the anceps position before the caesura

Iam nē tardēris: *Now do not delay*; subj. in a negative command

Commiscēre ... nōbīscum: *be joined with us willingly*; *commiscēre* is a pass.
  imperative used as an euphemism for sexual intercourse

dētestēris, lapidēris: pres. subj. in a future less vivid conditional

Ō malus ambōrum cōnsēnsus et impiger hōrum,   105

Quō sunt cōnātī pariter viciōsius ūtī.

Perpetuō dignae meritīs sānctaeque Susannae

Perstābant caecī simul in prece valde tenācī,

Illa sed inmobilis nec in hōrum vōta reclīnis

Perdūrat, Dominō spem pōnēns prīncipe summō,   110

In sē spērantēs quī dat cito congratulantēs.

---

ambō, -ae, -ō: both

caecus, -a, -um: blind

cōnor (1): try, attempt

cōnsēnsus, -ūs m.: agreement

inmōbilis (= immōbilis), -e:
 unmoved; immovable

impiger, impigra, impigrum:
 quick

pariter: likewise, at the same time

perdūrō (1): hold out, endure;
 make hard, harden

perpetuō (adv.): constantly,
 forever

perstō, -āre, -stitī, -stātum:
 continue standing; remain fixed;
 persist

prex, precis f.: prayer, request

prīnceps, -cipis: foremost,
 distinguished

reclīnis, -e: leaning back, inclined

tenāx, -ācis: persistent, obstinate

valdē: strongly

viciōsus (CL: vitiōsus), -a, -um:
 faulty, wicked

Quō ... ūtī: *cōnsēnsus* is antecedent; *quō* is the abl. object of *ūtī*, a deponent inf.

viciōsius: comp. adv.

dignae ... caecī: *blind to the merits of worthy and holy Susanna*

Susannae = *Sūsannae*; see note on line 16 of the prologue

valde = *valdē*; W. treats the *e* as short for the meter

inmobilis = *inmōbilis*; W. treats the *o* as short for the meter

In ... congratulantēs: see note on line 97

congratulantēs = *congrātulantēs*; W. treats the first *a* as short for the meter

Sīc quoque, nōn nactī tunc effectum malefactī,

Altera vīpereīs īnstaurant arma venēnīs,

Vōceque perversā prōmunt haec scīlicet ōrsa.

Hīc nunc offēnsa: "Fac quod vult iussio nostra,   115

Quod sī nōlueris forsan turbābere falsīs.

Dīcēmus iuvenem tēcum vīdisse iocantem,

Proptereāque duās hinc tē mīsisse puellās."

---

effectus, –ūs m.: effect, result

falsum, –ī n.: untruth, falsehood

forsan (adv.): perhaps

īnstaurō (1): renew; establish

iocor (1): joke, play, flirt

iussiō, –ōnis f.: order, command

iuvenis, –enis m.: youth

malefactum, –ī n.: evil deed

nancīscor, –ī, nanctus sum:
 obtain

offēnsa, –ae f.: offense, affront

ōrsa, –ōrum n.pl.: words, speech

perversus, –a, –um: perverse,
 wicked

prōmō, –ere, prōmpsī,
 prōmptum: bring forth; say

proptereā: therefore, for this
 reason

scīlicet (adv.): certainly, that is to
 say

turbō (1): disturb, trouble

venēnum, –ī n.: venom; drug

vīpereus, –a, –um: viperous,
 malignant

Altera ... venēnīs: *They resort to alternate weapons with viperous venoms*

Vōceque perversā: abl. of manner

Hīc ... offēnsa: *Here [and] now [is] the offense*

offēnsa: the short nom. ending falls in the anceps position before the caesura

iussio = *iussiō*; W. treats the *o* as short for the meter

nōlueris ... turbābere: fut. perf. indicatives in a future more vivid conditional;
 turbābere = *turbāberis*

Exemplō digna cūnctīs referenda Susanna

In biviō stricta, quia morsū crīminis icta,   120

Ingemit ex cordē, fundēns haec dulcius ōre:

---

bivium, -ī n.: crossroad

exemplum, -ī n.: example, model

fundō, -ere, fūdī, fūsum: pour

īciō, -ere, īcī, ictum: strike

ingemō, -ere, -uī, -itum: groan

morsus, -ūs m.: bite

stringō, -ere, strīnxī, strictum: draw tight; bind fast; press

---

Exemplō digna: *worthy of [being an] example*

digna: the short nom. ending falls in the anceps position before the caesura

Susanna = *Sūsanna*; see note on line 16 of the prologue

stricta: the short nom. ending falls in the anceps position before the caesura

crīminis: *of accusation*

dulcius: comp. adv.

"Angustor nimium, faciam quid et īnscia prīmum;

Ēgero sī forte, mē perpetuā neco morte;

Nēque manūs prāvās fugiam, sī dēnego, vestrās.

Sed mihi sit mālle vestrum mē spernere velle, 125

Quam cum peccātō vestrō mē subdere vōtō."

---

angustō (1): make narrow, straiten

dēnegō (1): reject, refuse

ēgerō, –ere, –gessī, –gestum: carry out, do

īnscius, –a, –um: not knowing

necō (1): kill, destroy

nimium (adv.): excessively

peccātum, –ī n.: sin

perpetuus, –a, –um: continuous

prāvus, –a, –um: crooked, perverse

spernō, –ere, sprēvī, sprētum: reject

subdō, –ere, –didī, –ditum (+dat.): submit

---

faciam … prīmum: rearrange: *et īnscia [sum] quid faciam prīmum*; *faciam* is a deliberative subjunctive in an indirect question

Ēgero = *ēgerō*; W. treats the *o* as short for the meter

forte: the final syllable falls in the anceps position before the caesura

neco = *necō*; W. treats the *o* as short for the meter

Nēque = *neque*; W. treats the first *e* as long for the meter

dēnego = *dēnegō*; W. treats the *o* as short for the meter

Sed … velle: *But, for me, let it be preferable that I reject your desire*

mihi sit mālle = *mālim* (pres. subj. of *malō* "prefer")

mālle: the final syllable falls in the anceps position before the caesura

mē: acc. subject of spernere

velle = *voluntātem* (acc. sg. of *voluntās*), modified by *vestrum*

Quam: *rather than*; comparative particle with *mihi sit mālle*

cum peccātō: abl. of manner

mē subdere: *mē* functions both as the acc. subject and the reflexive direct object of the inf.

Iam magis inde dolēns, viciō subcumbere nōlēns,

Vōce quidem magnā tunc clāmitat alma Susanna,

Adversusque piam conclāmant oppido nēquam.

Pectore cum fīdō pugnābat et ātra libīdo.   130

Nunc precibus fūsīs dabo vōbīs prōmere Mūsīs,

Quālēs cōnflīctūs faceret cum crīmine virtūs,

Aut mala quō vastā caderent virtūtis in hastā,

Et reserāte foris quid ferveat intus amōris.

āter, atra, atrum: black, dark

clāmitō (1): cry aloud

conclāmō (1): cry out together

cōnflīctus, -ūs m.: fight, clash

doleō, -ēre, -uī, -itum: grieve

fīdus, -a, -um: faithful,
 trustworthy

forīs (adv.): outwardly, without

fundō, -ere, fūdī, fūsum: pour

hasta, -ae f.: spear

intus (adv.): inwardly, within

libīdo, -inis f.: passion, lust

Mūsa, -ae f.: Muse

nēquam (indeclinable):
 worthless, wicked

oppidō (adv.): very

prōmō, -ere, prōmpsī,
 prōmptum: bring forth; say

pugnō (1): fight

reserō (1): open, reveal

subcumbō (= succumbō), -ere,
 -cubuī, -cubitus (+dat.):
 succumb to

vāstus, -a, -um: empty, vast

vicium (CL: vitium), -iī n.:
 blemish, fault, sin, wickedness

Vōce … magnā: abl. of manner

oppido = *oppidō*; W. treats the final *o* as short for the meter

nēquam: take as the nom. subject of *conclāmant: wicked men*

dabo … Mūsīs: *I will grant to you, Muses, to say*

faceret, caderent: imperf. subj. in an indirect question

virtūs: nom. sg. subject of *faceret*

amōris: partitive gen. dependent on *quid*

Ōstia festīnus reserat tunc nāviter ūnus,   135
Et Ioachim famulī, seniōrum vel quoque dūlī,
Per postīca ruunt, quaenam sit causa requīrunt
Clāmōris tantī, quem exaudierant ibi cūnctī.

---

clāmor, -ōris m.: outcry, shout

dūlus, -ī m. (Grk. δοῦλος): slave, servant

exaudiō, -īre, -īvī, -ītum: hear

famulus, -ī m.: male house slave, servant

ferveō, -ēre, ferbuī: boil

festīnus, -a, -um: hasty

malum, -ī n.: evil, calamity

nāviter: actively, zealously, diligently

postīcum, -ī n.: back door

quisnam (quīnam), quaenam, quidnam: who indeed? what indeed?

requīrō, -ere, -quīsīvī, -quīsītum: seek

reserō (1): open, reveal

ruō, -ere, -ī, rūtum: rush

Ioachim: take as possessive gen.

vel = *et*

quaenam ... tantī: rearrange: *requīrunt quaenam sit causa clāmōris tantī*; *sit* is subj. in an indirect question

Dīcunt prespiterī iuvenem vīdisse iocārī
Comprēnsā domnā, quī mox hāc vōce nefandā   140
Cordetenus tāctī, quia tālis nūllibi factī
Audierant ictum dē sānctā hāc cōniuge dictum.

---

comprēndō (comprehendō),
  -ere, -predsī, -prensum: seize,
  apprehend; catch in the act
coniūnx, -iugis f.: spouse, wife
cordetenus (adv.): deep within
  one's heart
ictus, -ūs m.: blow, strike

iocor (1): joke, flirt
iuvenis, -enis m.: youth
nefandus, -a, -um: unspeakable
nūllibī (adv.): nowhere
prespiter (presbyter), -erī m.
  (Grk. πρεσβύτερος): elder
sānctus, -a, -um: venerable, holy

---

domnā: syncopated form of *dominā*
quī: *and they*; connective relative with *famulī* as the antecedent
tāctī: supply *sunt*
tālis ... factī: gen. of the charge

Āh, āh, Fāma, malum cuī nōn vēlōcius ūllum:
Trānsvolat ac statim diffāmat rem triviātim.
Quot maculās Scylla, mendātia tot gerit illa,   145
Huius et affīnēs facit undique convenientēs
Crīmen hoc incestī, quī plangunt intime maestī.

---

affīnis, -e: neighboring, related
 (esp. by marriage)
conveniō, -īre, -vēnī, ventum:
 convene, come together
diffāmō (1): divulge, make known
incestum, -ī n.: improper sexual
 relations
intime: deeply, inwardly
macula, -ae f.: spot; stain; blemish
maestus, -a, -um: sad, sorrowful
malum, -ī n.: evil, calamity
mendātium (CL: mendacium),
 -iī n.: lie

plangō, -ere, plānxī, planctum:
 beat; bewail
Scylla, -ae f.: Scylla, a
 sea-monster
statim (adv.): at once, immediately
transvolō (1): fly across
triviātim (adv.): everywhere,
 far and wide
undique (adv.): from every side,
 from everywhere
vēlōx, -ōcis: fast

Fāma … ūllum: cf. Vergil *Aen.* 4.174: *Fāma, malum quā nōn aliud vēlōcius ūllum*
cuī: dat. of comparison for expected *quā*, abl. of comparison
statim = *statim*; W. treats the *a* as long for the meter
Scylla: cf. lines 68–70; the short nom. ending falls in the anceps position before
 the caesura
illa: i.e., Susanna
Huius … incestī: rearrange: *hoc crīmen incestī facit affīnēs huius undique convenientēs*
convenientēs = *convenīre*, with *affīnēs* as acc. subject
incestī: gen. of the charge; here: *adultery*
intime = *intimē*; W. treats the *e* as short for the meter

Hōs etenim populus recolēns per cūncta benignus
Ante frequentābat, preciī quōs plūris habēbat,
Concordāns pariter mixtim cum dīvite pauper.   150
Pollēbant studiō dignī plūs omnibus ambō.

---

benignus, -a, -um: kind,
  generous
concordō (1): agree
frequentō (1): crowd together,
  frequent
mixtim (adv.): mixedly, together
pauper, -eris: poor
plūs (adv.): more; furthermore

pollēō, -ēre, —, —: be strong,
  prevail in (+abl.)
precium (CL: pretium), -ī n.:
  price, value
recolō, -ere, -uī, -cultum: till
  again, consider
studium, -iī n.: eagerness,
  devotion

Hōs: i.e., the elders; object of *ante*
preciī ... plūris: gen. of value
ambō: substantive: *both men*

Scīlicet affīnēs sibi conciliārier omnēs
Ac sibi concīvēs prōrsus cōnstāre fidēlēs
Quod signat, plūrēs quibus istaec corde dolet rēs.

---

affīnis, -e: neighboring, related
 (esp. by marriage)
conciliō (1): reconcile, win over
concīvis, -is m.: fellow-citizen
cōnstō (1): agree
doleō, -ēre, -uī, -itum: feel pain,
 grieve on account of

fidēlis, -e: faithful
istic, istaec, istoc: this very
prōrsus (adv.): forwards; truly
scīlicet (adv): of course, to be
 sure, doubtless
signō (1): signify, mark, mean

---

affīnēs: i.e., her relatives by marriage; cf. *cognātīs* (her blood relatives) in line 167

conciliārier = *conciliārī*

conciliārier, cōnstāre: the infinitives here work like an indirect statement after
 scīlicet, which often introduces an explanation; translate as finite verbs

Quod: indefinite antecedent

signat: scribal gloss: *scīlicet infāmia eius dē incestū suō* (*evidently, her disgrace from her
 adultery*)

plūrēs: substantive: *many people*; antecedent of *quibus*

istaec: agrees with *rēs*; scribal gloss: *id est ista* (*that is, "ista" [that]*)

dolet: here with the meaning "to cause pain"

Ecce sequente diē prīmum dēcernitur hāc rē: 155

Convēnit populus, discussor crīminis huius,

Inque domō Ioachim glomerātur turba virītim.

Adsunt et prāvī prāvō meditāmine plēnī,

Bīnī prespiterī, fraudantēs fāmina vērī,

Quī dīcunt populīs per eōrum iussa vocātīs: 160

---

bīnī, -ae, -a: two by two, two

conveniō, -īre, -vēnī, -ventum:
  convene, assemble

dēcernō, -ere, -crēvī, -crētum:
  determine, settle

discussor, -ōris m.: judge

fāmen, -inis n.: utterance, speech

fraudō (1): defraud

glomerō (1): form into a ball, mass

iūssum, -ī n.: command, order

meditāmen, -inis n.: thought,
  plan

virītim (adv.): one by one

Ioachim: take as possessive gen.

glomerātur: scribal gloss: *id est congregātur* (*that is, they are gathered*)

prāvī prāvō meditāmine plēnī: *depraved and full of depraved thought*; chiasmus

fraudantēs: scribal gloss: *id est menciēbantur* (CL = *mentiēbantur*) (*that is, they were lying*)

populīs ... vocātīs: abl. absolute or dat. indirect object of *dīcunt*

"Mittite Sūsannam, quam nōscimus, āh, male dignam
Ad sociam Ioachim, quam nōs dīlēximus ōlim.
Helchīae nātam per iūra vocāte necandam."
Mox quoque mīsērunt Sūsannam sīcque vocārunt,
Quae bene fīrmāta Dominī spē nīlque morāta,   165
Ōrāns cum psalmīs, comitāta parentibus almīs
Ac sibi cognātīs cum cūnctīs vel sibi nōtīs,
Prōmptius accelerat, simul hūc pervēnit et intrat.

---

accelerō (1): hasten

cognātus, –ī m.: relative (male)

dīligō, –ere, –lēxī, –lēctum: cherish, hold dear

fīrmō (1): strengthen

Helchīa, –ae m.: Helchia, father of Susanna

hūc (adv.): to this place, hither

intrō (1): enter

moror (1): delay

necō (1): kill

olim (adv.): formerly, once

orō (1): pray

prōmptus, –a, –um: ready, quick

psalmus, –ī m.: psalm

socia, –ae f.: companion, spouse

---

male dignam: *unworthy*

Ad sociam: in ML, *ad* with an acc. may replace the dat. with adjectives like *aptus* and *idōneus*. W. seems to be using the same construction with the adjective *dignam* in the previous line.

Ioachim: take as possessive gen.

necandam: fut. pass. participle expressing purpose with *vocāte*

vocārunt = *vocāvērunt*

fīrmāta: the short nom. ending falls in the anceps position before the caesura

cognātīs: i.e., her blood relatives; cf. *affīnēs* (her relatives by marriage) in line 152

nōtīs: substantive: *friends*

Omnis dēflet eam, quisquis cognōverat illam.

Hīc quoque presbiterī, quīs lēx in lēge verērī   170

Altithronum Dominum, sed ab illīs tunc male sprētum,

Iussērunt tollī vestēs dē corpore mollī,

---

altithronus, -a, -um: throned on high

dēfleō, -ēre, -flēvī, -flētum: weep over

spernō, -ere, sprēvī, sprētum: disdain, scorn

tollō, -ere, sustulī, sublātum: remove

vereor, -ērī, veritus sum: revere, fear

---

quīs: scribal gloss: *prō quibus* (*for whom*)

lēx in lēge: *law within Law* (i.e., a precept contained in the greater body of divine or canonical law)

verērī: subject inf.; supply *est*

sprētum: modifies *Dominum*

Iussērunt … mollī: In Ezekiel 16:37–39, the penalty for adultery includes being stripped naked and publicly shamed. Cf. Daniel 13:32, which implies only her veil was taken away: *At inīquī illī iussērunt ut discooperīrētur (erat enim cooperta) … (And those wicked men ordered that she be uncovered [for she was covered (i.e., veiled)] …)*

Ac vīsū dignae violant pudibunda Susannae,

Quō mēns prāvāta cōnspectū sit saciāta.

Ō male perversī, peius post pessima versī,   175

Quid fuerat mentis haec huius nūda videntis?

Vīvere numque libet sī mēns haec cernere vītet?

Nōn pudet hanc, ūllum Factor quō vestit homullum.

---

cōnspiciō, -ere, -spexī,
  -spectum: catch sight of, gaze

factor, -ōris m.: maker

homullus, -ī m.: little man,
  mortal

libet (libēre), libuit, libitum est:
it pleases, is pleasing (impers.)

nūdus, -a, -um: nude, stripped

pervertō, -ere, -ī, -sum: overturn,
  be turned the wrong way

pravō (1): make wicked or corrupt

pudeō, -ēre, -uī, -itum: make
  ashamed (impers.)

pudibunda, -orum n.pl.: private
  parts

saciō (CL: satiō) (1): satisfy

vestiō, -īre, -iī/īvī, -ītum: clothe

violō (1): violate, violate sexually

vīsus, -ūs m.: sight

vītō (1): avoid, shun

---

pubibunda: lit., "the things about which one ought to be modest"

prāvāta: the short nom. ending falls in the anceps position before the caesura

cōnspectū: abl. supine

sit: potential subj. or subj. in a purpose clause introduced by *quō*

Quid…videntis: *What were you thinking, looking upon the nude body of this
  woman?* (lit., *What had been of [your] mind, seeing these nude things [i.e.,
  pudibunda] of this woman?*)

numque = *nōnne* (introducing a question expecting a positive answer)

Quod nātūra dedit, sat in illō quīvis habēbit.

Quid vōbīs dīcam mentem ut dētester inīquam?   180

Prō meritīs dignīs vōbīs cito dēbeat ignis!

Tunc pariter surgunt, quia factum dīcere pergunt.

In mediō populī nam cōnsēdēre curūlī,

Inpōnuntque manūs iūrando super caput eius.

---

cōnsīdō, –ere, –sēdī, –sessum: sit
  down
curūlis, –is f.: curule chair, official
  chair
dētestor (1): denounce, condemn
inīquus, –a, –um: uneven; sinful
iūrō (1): swear, conspire

medium, –iī n.: middle
pergō, –ere, –rēxī, –rēctum:
  proceed
quīvīs, quaevīs, quodvīs: anyone,
  anything
sat (adv.): enough
surgō, –ere, –rēxī, –rēctum: rise

---

in illō: antecedent to *quod*

quīvis = *quīvīs*; W. treats the second *i* as short for the meter

dīcam: subj. in a deliberative question

Prō ... ignis: scribal gloss: *ignem īnfernālem dignē meruistis (you have appropriately
  deserved hellfire)*

dēbeat: jussive or optative subj. with *ignis* as its subject

ignis: scribal gloss: *īnfernālis (of Hell)*

cōnsēdēre = *cōnsēdērunt*

iūrando: abl. gerund used adverbially to show attendant circumstance (see
  section IV of the introduction for W.'s use of abl. gerunds); W. treats the final *o*
  as short for the meter

Quae flēns pernimium satagēbat cernere caelum,   185

Et fuit in Dominō cor fīdēns intime Chrīstō,

In sē spērantēs quī dat cito congratulantēs.

At criticī versī dīxērunt, tāliter ōrsī:

"Fortuitū sōlī cum nōs incessimus hērī

Huius pōmeriō, domuī quod subiacet, ergō   190

Vēnerat haec bīnīs tantum comitāta puellīs,

---

bīnī, -ae, -a: two by two, two

caelus, -ī m.: sky, heavens

criticus, -ī m.: judge

fīdō, -ere, fīsus sum: trust, believe

fortuitū (adv.): by chance

herī (adv.): yesterday, here

incēdō, -ere, -cessī, -cessum: go; proceed; walk (in a stately manner)

intimē: deeply, inwardly

ōrdior, -īrī, ōrsus sum: begin

pernimium (adv.): far too much; very much

satagō, -ere, -ēgī, -āctum: be busy with, endeavor

subiaceō, -ēre, -uī (+dat.): lie under, lie near

tāliter (adv.): in such a way, thus

Quae: *And she*; connective relative

intime = *intimē*; W. treats the *e* as short for the meter

In … congratulantēs: see note on line 97

congratulantēs = *congrātulantēs*; W. treats the first *a* as short for the meter

criticī: scribal gloss: *Crēticus dīcitur iūdex, inde criticī vel cretecī dīcuntur iūdicēs in linguā latīnā* (a judge is called a "creticus," hence judges are called "critici" or "creteci" in the Latin language)

versī, ōrsī: perf. pass. participles both modifying the nom. subject *criticī*

cum … incessimus: temporal *cum* clause

hērī = *herī*; W. treats the *e* as long for the meter

Huius: i.e., of Joachim

Ēmittēnsque suās stātim per verba puellās

Ōstia pōmeriī iussit cum vecte serārī.

Hic tunc prōsiliēns compresserat hanc adolēscēns,

Quod nōs cernentēs fuimus prope forte latentēs.   195

Gressū festīnō mox illō vēnimus ambō.

Cum pervēnerimus, iam commiscēre vidēmus.

---

adulēscēns, -entis: youth

commisceō, -ēre, -uī, -mixtum: mix together; blend, mingle

comprimō, -ere, -pressī, -pressum: press together

ēmittō, -ere, -mīsī, -mīssum: send out

festīnus, -a, -um: hasty

gressus, -ūs m.: step

illō (adv.): to there

lateō, -ēre, -uī: lie hidden, be hidden

prōsiliō, -īre, -uī: leap or spring forth

serō (1): fasten with a bolt, bar

statim (adv.): at once, immediately

vectis, vectis m.: pole, lever, bar, bolt

---

stātim = *statim*; W. treats the *a* as long for the meter

compresserat: verbs of pressing are often used to describe sexual activity

Gressū festīnō: abl. of manner

Cum pervēnerimus: circumstantial *cum* clause

pervēnerimus = *pervēnerīmus*; W. treats the *i* as short for the meter

commiscēre: a euphemism for sexual activity; supply *eōs* as subject acc. in indirect statement

Intereā iuvenem cito portās tunc reserantem

Prēndere nōn quīmus, nam fortior nostri relāpsus.

Hanc etenim prēnsam rogitāmus: Dīc homo quisnam!   200

Quae rogitāta negāns negat haec ēdīcere cōnstāns.

Huius nempe reī testēs sumus ōrdine vērī."

---

cōnstāns, –antis: steadfast, sure

ēdīcō, –ere, –dīxī, –dictum: make known, proclaim

iuvenis, –enis m.: youth

nempe (adv.): indeed, to be sure

ōrdō, –inis m.: narrative, account

prēndō (prehendō), –ere, –ī, –sum (+gen./acc.): snatch, seize

queō, quīre, quīvī/quiī, quitum: be able

quisnam (quīnam), quaenam, quidnam: who indeed? what indeed?

relābor, relābī, relāpsus sum: slip back; retreat

reserō (1): unlock, open

rogitō (1): keep asking, question

testis, –is m.: witness

---

fortior: W. treats the final *o* as short, although it is long by position

nostri = *nostrī*; W. treats the *i* as short for the meter; gen. of comparison in imitation of ancient Greek

relāpsus: supply *est*

Dīc ... quisnam: supply *sit*, subj. in an indirect question

homo = *homō*; W. treats the final *o* as short for the meter

Quae: *And she*; connective relative

Huius reī: objective gen. dependent on *testēs*

testēs ... vērī: *vērī* is an adjective agreeing with *tēstēs*: *faithful witnesses in [our] account of this matter*

Hīs igitur dictīs populus mox crēdidit istīs,

Ut senibus sēnsū mātūrīs scīlicet āctū.

Prōh dolor! Hanc sortem, sānxērunt huic male mortem,   205

Sed fortūna magis facit hoc quam tū, Deus orbis;

Dum caro vīxistī, fortūnam tūque subistī,

Gustandō mortem, cūnctīs reparando salūtem.

āctus, –ūs m.: act

carō, carnis f.: meat, flesh

dictum, –ī n.: word; saying

intereā (adv.): meanwhile, (ML) at this time

gustō (1): taste

mātūrus, –a, –um: ripe; mature

porta, –ae f.: gate, entrance

prōh (prō) (interj.): O! Alas!

reparō (1): get again, restore, renew

salūs, –ūtis f.: safety; salvation

sanciō, –īre, sānxī, sānctum: decree; ordain

subeō, –īre, –īvī/iī, –itum: go under; endure

Ut: *as*; adverbial *ut*

sēnsū, āctū: abl. of respect with *mātūrīs*

scīlicet āctū: *supposedly in their conduct*; *scīlicet* is used ironically here

Sed ... orbis: scribal gloss: *scīlicet quod crēditur senibus* (*evidently because the elders are believed*)

caro = *carō*; W. treats the *o* as short for the meter

Gustandō, reparando: abl. gerunds used adverbially to express attendant circumstance (see section IV of the introduction for W.'s use of abl. gerunds); W. treats the *o* of *reparando* as short for the meter

Ō mala fortūna, numquam stāns sorte sub ūnā,
Omnia sed vergēns ac cūncta potentia mergēns,   210
Alta vel īma tuīs semper facis affore lūdīs,
Parcere nec dignae saltim dignāta Susannae,
Quam magis īnsontem fīnxistī nunc fore sontem.

---

dignor (1): deign; deem fit

fingō, -ere, fīnxī, fīctum: mold,
  shape; create, invent

īmus, -a, -um: lowest, deepest

īnsōns, -ontis: innocent, guiltless

lūdus, -ī m.: game, sport, trick

mergō, -ere, mersī, mersum: dip,
  sink, overwhelm, cover

parcō, -ere, pepercī, parcitus
  (+dat.): spare, preserve

potēns, potentis: powerful,
  strong; mighty

saltim (adv.): at least, at any rate

sōns, sontis: hurtful; guilty;
  criminal

vergō, -ere, —, —: incline; bend;
  sink

---

fortūna: the short vocative ending falls in the anceps position before the caesura

affore: fut. inf. of *adsum*, dependent on *facis*: *you cause to take part in* (+dat.)

Parcere: complementary inf. with *dignāta*

Susannae = *Sūsannae*; see note on line 16 of the prologue

Quam: relative pronoun with *Susannae* as its antecedent

fore: fut. inf. of *sum*, dependent on *fīnxistī*: *you shaped to be*

Dīxerat ast altē lacrimāns Sūsanna gemēnsque:
"Ō Deus aeterne, rēgnātor summus in arce   215
Aulae caelestis, alme et tū conditor orbis,
Cognitor occultī, factor simul inclite mundī,
Pernōscēns cūncta quam sint, Deus, ante futūra.

---

aeternus, -a, -um: eternal,
  everlasting
altē: aloft; high; deeply
arx, arcis f.: citadel, height
aula, -ae f.: court, hall; palace
caelestis, -e: from/of heaven
cognitor, -ōris m.: one with
  knowledge
conditor, -ōris m.: founder
factor, -ōris m.: maker, doer
gemō, -ere, -uī: groan, sigh

inclitus, -a, -um: famous,
  glorious, renowned
lacrimō (1): cry, weep
mundus, -ī m.: world, universe,
  heavens
occultus, -a, -um: hidden, secret
pernōscō, -ere, -nōvī, -nōtum:
  know thoroughly
rēgnātor, -ōris m.: sovereign,
  lord

---

ast = *at*

aeterne: the final syllable falls in the anceps position before the caesura

Pernōscēns … futūra: rearrange: *Deus, pernōscēns cūncta antequam futūra sint*

cūncta: the final syllable falls in the anceps position before the caesura

Tū scīs, ō Domine, falsum collīditur in mē,
Ecce quidem pereō, vītā et sine mōre carēbō, 220
Nīl faciēns hōrum, nec cōnscia compositōrum."
Invocat hoc nōmen. Quam māgnum perferat ōmen!
Exauditque Deus vōcem pie dēsuper eius,

---

careō, -ēre, -uī, -itus (+abl.):
lack, be without, be free from
collīdō, -ere, -līsī, -līsum: clash,
strike, crush
compōnō, -ere, -posuī,
-positum: build; invent, contrive
cōnscius, -a, -um (+gen.): having
knowledge, aware
desuper (adv.): from above, on
high

exaudiō, -īre, -īvī, -ītum: hear
falsum, -ī n.: untruth, falsehood
invocō (1): invoke, call upon
ōmen, -inis n.: power, omen
perferō, -ferre, -tulī, -lātum:
carry, bring, convey

Domine: the final syllable falls in the anceps position before the caesura
collīditur = *collīdī*
vītā et = *et vītā*
sine mōre: *wrongfully, in violation of custom*
hōrum: partitive gen. dependent on *Nīl*
perferat: optative subj.; take *nōmen* as the subject
pie = *piē*; W. treats the *e* as short for the meter; *mercifully*

Ut pius indultor aut aeque salūtis amātor,

In sē spērantēs quī dat cito congratulantēs.   225

Rēgnum caeleste valet hīc perpendere quisque

Afflīctī cordis vel pūrae vōx pia mentis

Aut tāctus sī quis vel cūrīs mactus inīquīs.

---

aequē: equally

amātor, –ōris m.: lover

caelestis, –e: heavenly

indultor, –ōris m.: supporter

inīquus, –a, –um: uneven; unjust

mactō (1): sacrifice, punish, ruin

perpendō, –ere, –pendī, –pēnsum: examine

pūrus, –a, –um: pure, clean

salūs, –ūtis f.: safety; deliverance, salvation

valeō, –ēre, –uī, –itum: be strong, be able

---

pius: in ML, *pius* can mean "benevolent" or "merciful" when applied to God or Christ (cf. *pie* in line 223)

indultor: the final syllable falls in the anceps position before the caesura

aeque = *aequē*; W. treats the *e* as short for the meter

In ... congratulantēs: see note on line 97

congratulantēs = *congrātulantēs*; W. treats the first *a* as short for the meter

caeleste: the final syllable falls in the anceps position before the caesura

hīc: i.e., *here on Earth*

tāctus, mactus: supply *est*

quis = *aliquis*

mactus = *mactātus*

Quam pernīx aurēs pertingat adūsque perhennēs,
Dē quō Psalmista dēclāmāns addidit ista: 230
"Cor tū contrītum, Deus ō, nōn spernis initum
Spīritus ac grātus tibi cōnstāt contribulātus."

---

adūsque (adv.): entirely

cōnstō (1): stand, exist

contrībulō (1): crush, bruise

contrītus, -a, -um: contrite, humble

dēclāmō (1): speak, declaim

initio (1): begin; initiate

perhennis (CL: perennis), -e: eternal, everlasting

pernīx, -īcis: swift, agile

pertingō, -ere, -tigī, -tāctum: extend

psalmista, -ae m: composer or singer of psalms; Psalmist (i.e., King David)

spernō, -ere, sprēvī, sprētum: reject, spurn

spīritus, -ūs m.: breath, spirit; the Holy Spirit

---

pertingat: optative or potential subj.

Psalmista: the short nom. ending falls in the anceps position before the caesura

"Cor ... contribulātus.": cf. Psalm 50:19: *Sacrificium Deō spīritus contrībulātus; cor contrītum et humiliātum, Deus, nōn dēspiciēs. (A troubled spirit is a sacrifice to God; a contrite and humbled heart, God, you will not despise.)*

initum = *initātum; initiated* (i.e., baptized)

contribulātus = *contrībulātus*; W. treats the *i* as short for the meter

Quod verbum digna recolēns in mente Susanna

Tē bene contrīta, Deus, invocat ac tribulāta,

Quam pius exaudīs clēmenter, tū Deus orbis,   235

Verbere quī tāctum tibi māvīs esse perāctum.

---

clēmenter: mercifully

contrītus, -a, -um: contrite, humble

exaudiō, -īre, -īvī, -ītum: hear

invocō (1): invoke, call upon

peragō, -ere, -ēgī, -āctum: finish, prosecute until a defendant is condemned

recolō, -ere, -uī, -cultum: call to mind, contemplate

trībulō (1): oppress, afflict

verber, -eris n.: whip; blow

---

digna: the short nom. ending falls in the anceps position before the caesura

Susanna = *Sūsanna*; see note on line 16 of the prologue

contrīta: the short nom. ending falls in the anceps position before the caesura

tribulāta = *trībulāta*; W. treats the *i* as short for the meter

Quam: relative pronoun with *Susanna* as its antecedent

pius: see note on *pius* in line 224

Verbere ... perāctum.: *You who prefer that [one] be struck by a whip* (i.e., punished) *[and] condemned by you*; *tibi* is a dat. of agent

esse: take with both *tāctum* and *perāctum*

Dūcitur ad mortem tōtam comitāta cohortem,
Martyrium mente complēns vītāque manēnte
Perpetuō digna celebrī sub sorte Susanna.
Spīritus at Dominī tunc illapsus iuniōrī   240
Iūdiciō plēnum puerō quī fēcerat aevum,
Nōmine quī Daniēl, clāmāns tantummodo sēmel,
Dīxerat hoc verbum clārē dīvīnitus haustum:

---

celeber, -bris, -bre: renowned,
 famous
clāmō (1): proclaim, cry out
cohors, -ortis f.: crowd, cohort
compleō, -ēre, -plēvī, -plētum:
 fill (up/in); occupy
Daniēl (indeclinable): Daniel
dīvīnitus (adv.): by divine
 inspiration
hauriō, -īre, hausī, haustum:
 draw

illābor, -ī, illāpsus sum (+dat.):
 flow into
iūdicium, -iī n.: judgment
iūnior, -ius: younger
martyrium, -iī n: martyrdom
perpetuō (adv.): constantly,
 forever
semel (adv.): once (one time)
tantummodo (adv.): only
vīta, -ae f.: (eternal) life

---

tōtam ... cohortem = *tōtā cohorte*; acc. in place of expected abl. to maintain the
 rhyme scheme
mente: the final syllable falls in the anceps position before the caesura
digna: the short nom. ending falls in the anceps position before the caesura
Susanna = *Sūsanna*; see note on line 16 of the prologue
Spīritus ... aevum: rearrange: *At spīritus Dominī tunc illapsus [est] iūniōrī puerō, quī*
 fēcerat aevum plēnum iūdiciō
iuniōrī = *iūniōrī*; W. treats the *u* as short for the meter
sēmel = *semel*; W. treats the first *e* as long for the meter

"Ēn ego sum mundus dampnātū sanguinis huius."

Hōc verbō cūnctī velut audīvēre morātī,   245

Omnis et hoc populus respondīt huic velut ūnus:

"Quō venit hic sermō, loqueris quem tū puer ergō?"

Tunc stāns in mediō Daniēl ait ōre pudīcō:

---

dampnō (CL: damnō) (1): find
  guilty, condemn

ēn: Behold!

moror (1): delay, linger

mundus, -a, -um: clean, pure,
  innocent, not guilty

pudīcus, -a, -um: modest,
  virtuous

respondeō, -ēre, -ī, -sum:
  respond, answer

sermō, -ōnis m.: speech

"Ēn...huius.": cf. Daniel 13:46: *Mundus ego sum ā sanguine huius.* (*I am clean from the blood of this woman.*)

dampnātū: abl. supine with *mundus* (*innocent of the condemnation*); governs the objective gen. *sanguinis*

Hōc verbō: dat. with *audīvēre* (*they listened to this utterance*)

velut: take with *mōrātī*

audīvēre = *audīvērunt*

morātī: scribal gloss: *id est stupefactī* (*that is, stunned*)

ergō: here used in a question to signal that an explanation or clarification is being requested

"Israel ō genitī, datur hīc ut cernere stultī,

Iūdiciō prāvī, nūllō discrīmine vērī.   250

Quam male dampnāstis nātam nunc Israel istīs,

Cum potius plēbēs veniant hūc, quās movet haec rēs,

Presbiterōs istōs quō iam dīiūdicet ambōs."

Illico conversī cōnsīdunt, sunt ubi iussī,

Inquit et hīc Daniēl, cui rōrāt Spīritus hoc mel: 255

---

cōnsīdō, –ere, –sēdī, –sessum: sit
 down
convertō, –ere, –ī, –sum: turn
 around, retreat
dīiūdicō (1): judge by
 discernment, determine;
 condemn
discrīmen, –inis n.: discernment
gignō, –ere, genuī, genitum:
 beget

hūc (adv.): to this place, hither
īllicō (īlicō) (adv.): at once
mel, mellis n.: honey
plēbs, plēbis f.: common people
potius (adv.): rather, instead
rōrō (1): drip, drop, trickle
rēs, reī f.: case, matter, trial
stultus, –a, –um: foolish, stupid,
 slow-witted
vērum, –ī n.: truth

Israel: indeclinable, take as abl. of source

datur: *it is evident*; the subject of this verb is the following substantive *ut* clause

ut: substantive clause; supply *sītis*

cernere: explanatory (epexegetical) inf. dependent on *stultī*

Iūdiciō prāvī: *crooked in (your) judgment*; abl. of respect

nūllō discrīmine: abl. of description; governs the objective gen. *vērī*

dampnāstis = *dampnāvistis*

istīs: dat. of advantage; scribal gloss: *scilicet presbiterīs (namely, the elders)*

cum …veniant: subj. within a concessive *cum* clause

quō … dīiūdicet: purpose clause; take *plēbēs* (= sg. *plēbs*) as subject

Presbiterōs … dīiūdicet: *where they may now condemn both those elders*

Illico = *Illicō*; W. treats the *o* as short for the meter

"Longē dīversī statuantur crīmine mersī,

Dōnec convincam rabiem meditāminis uncam."

Quī mox dīvīsī sunt plūs mūtīre nec ausī,

Ūnus ut oblātus, Daniēl huic est ita fātus:

---

convincō, -ere, -vīcī, -victum:
  prove, demonstrate, convict

dīversus, -a, -um: separate, apart

dīvidō, -ere, -vīsī, -vīsum:
  divide; separate

for, fārī, fātus: speak, say

meditāmen, -inis n.: thought

mergō, -ere, mersī, mersum:
  immerse, overwhelm, involve

mūtiō, -īre, -īvī, -ītum: mumble

offerō, -ferre, obtulī, -lātum:
  present; bring before

plūs (adv.): more; furthermore

rabiēs, -ēī f.: madness

statuō, -ere, -ī, -tum: set up,
  establish

uncus, -a, -um: hooked, curved,
  bent

---

statuantur: jussive subj.

meditāminis: scribal gloss: *id est meditāciōnis* (CL = *meditātiōnis*) (*that is,*
  "meditacionis" [*of thought*])

uncam: scribal gloss: *id est falsam* (*that is, deceitful*)

Quī: *And they* (i.e., the elders); connective relative

plūs … ausī: rearrange: *nec plūs mūtīre ausī* [*sunt*]

Ūnus ut oblātus: temporal clause; supply *est*

"Iam scelus antīquum, caput inveterāte malōrum,   260
Pervenient in tē quae tū malus ēgeris ante,
Dampnāns innocuōs, dīmittēns atque nocīvōs,
Sīc dīcente Deō, cui servit caelicus ōrdō,
Īnsontem iūstum perimī tē iūdice nūllum.

---

antīquus, -a, -um: old, ancient
caelicus, -a, -um: of or from
  heaven
dampnō (CL: damnō) (1): find
  guilty, condemn
dīmittō, -ere, -mīsī, -mīssum:
  send away; set free
innocuus, -a, -um: harmless
īnsōns, -ontis: innocent

inveterātus, -a, -um: inveterate,
  old
nocīvus, -a, -um: hurtful,
  injurious
ōrdō, -inis m.: order
perimō, -ere, -ēmī, -ēmptum:
  destroy; kill
serviō, -īre, -īvī, -ītum (+dat.):
  serve

---

scelus ... inveterāte: voc.; *inveterāte* modifies the understood masc. elder rather
  than the neut. *caput*
caput ... malōrum: *source of evils*
quae: relative pronoun with indefinite antecedent (*the things which…*); subject of
  Pervenient
ēgeris: perf. subj. in a relative clause of characteristic
perimī: inf. in an indirect statement dependent on *dīcente Deō*
tē iūdice: abl. absolute

Nunc sī vīdistī, patulum dīc quod bene nōstī   265
Arbore sub quānam sibi fārī vīderis hōsnam?"
Quī cito respondēns: "Sub cīnō," dīxerat audēns.
Et Daniēl iūstus, cui dictat verbula Chrīstus:
"Hoc quia mentīris, Orcum peritūrus adībis.
Angelus ecce Deī plēctēns tē verbere vērī   270
Scindet tē medium, compēnsāns hoc tibi factum."

---

adeō, -īre, -īvī/iī, -itum:
  approach
angelus, -ī m.: messenger, angel
cīnus, -ī f. (Grk. σχῖνος): mastic
  tree
compensō (1): balance, weigh
dictō (1): assert repeatedly; dictate
for (1): speak, say
mentior, -īrī, mentītus sum: lie
  (about)
Orcus, -ī m.: the lower world;
  hell; god of the underworld

patulus, -a, -um: broad, open
plectō, -ere, plexī, plexum: beat;
  punish
quīnam, quaenam, quodnam:
  who? which? what?
respondeō, -ēre, -ī, -sum:
  respond, answer
scindō, -ere, scidī, scissum: cut,
  rend, tear asunder
verber, -eris n.: whip
vērum, -ī n.: truth

---

patulum = *patulē*

nōstī = *nōvistī*

vīderis = *vīderis*; W. treats the second *i* as short for the meter; perf. subj. in an
  indirect question

hōsnam: the -*nam* here is a repetition of the emphatic interrogative enclitic from
  quānam; acc. subject of *fārī* in an indirect statement

Quī: *And he*; connective relative

verbula: diminutive of *verba*

mentīris: the final syllable falls in the anceps position before the caesura

compēnsāns ... factum: *balancing this deed against you*

Optime convictus sīc est mox iste remōtus,
Alter ut oblātus, Daniēl huic est ita fātus:
"Sēmen tū Canaān fallēnsque genus tibi Iūdam,
Tē male dēcēpit speciēs virtūsque relīquit,   275
Subvertitque tuum petulante cupīdine sēnsum.

Canaan (indeclinable): Canaan,
 father of the Canaanites
convincō, –ere, –vīcī, –vīctum:
 prove wrong, convict
cupīdō, –inis f.: desire, eagerness
dēcipiō, –ere, –cēpī, –ceptum:
 deceive, cheat, beguile
fallō, –ere, fefellī, falsum:
 deceive, betray
for (1): speak, say
genus, –eris n.: offspring,
 descendent
Iūdas, –ae m: Judah, son of
 Jacob; the tribe of Judah

nimis (adv.): very much;
 exceedingly
offerō, –ferre, obtulī, –lātum:
 present; bring before
optimus, –a, –um: best, excellent
petulāns, –antis: wanton
removeō, –ēre, –mōvī, –mōtum:
 remove
sēmen, –inis n.: seed
sēnsus, –ūs m.: feeling; sense,
 reason
speciēs, –ēī f.: appearance, beauty
subvertō, –ere, –ī, –sum: destroy,
 subvert

Optime = *Optimē*; W. treats the *e* as short for the meter
Alter ut oblātus: temporal clause; supply *est*
Sēmen ... Canaān: evokes the biblical tradition that the Canaanites were
 morally corrupt, idolatrous, and subject to Israel's judgment (cf. Genesis
 9:25–27); take *Canaan* as abl. of source
genus: vocative parallel to *Sēmen*
tibi: dat. of advantage with *fallēns*

Sīc faciēbātis vōs Israel undique nātīs,

Quae nimis āmentēs sunt vōbīs cūncta loquentēs.

Fīlia sed Iūdā numquam mala pertulit illa.

Haec quia dīxistī, patulum dīc, quod bene nōstī,   280

Arbore sub quānam, bone tū, comprēnderis hōsnam?"

āmēns, –entis: frantic, scared out
 of one's wits
comprēndō (comprehendō),
 –ere, –ī, –sum: seize, apprehend,
 observe
Iūdas, –ae m: Judah, son of Jacob;
 the tribe of Judah

patulus, –a, –um: broad, open
perferō, –ferre, –tulī, –lātum:
 bear, submit to, endure
quīnam, quaenam, quodnam:
 who? which? what?
undique (adv.): everywhere; all
 over

Israel: indeclinable; take as abl. of source with *nātīs*

nātīs: dat. of disadvantage with *faciēbātis*

cūncta = *cūnctae*; nom. pl. agreeing with *Quae*

loquentēs: possibly a euphemism for intimate contact, i.e., they were having
 relations with them

Iūdā: abl. of source

patulum = *patulē*

nōstī = *nōvistī*

comprēnderis = *comprēnderīs*; W. treats the *i* as short for the meter; perf. subj. in
 an indirect question

hōsnam: see note on *hōsnam* in line 266

Dīcēns "Sub prīnō," prōfert mendātia, prīmō

Cum prīnō tūtus, mānsūrus in ultima mūtus.

Tum puer hic sānctus ambōrum fāmine fūnctus,

Quō fit praeclārum cūnctīs prō crīmine vērum,   285

Respondēns clārē sīc huic maledīxit amārē:

"Haec quia mentīris, Orcum peritūrus adībis.

Angelus exurgēns iūstus tē iūstius urgēns

Ipsum tē medium gladiō secet ob malefactum."

---

adeō, -īre, -īvī/iī, -itum: approach

amārus, -a, -um: bitter; harsh

angelus, -ī m.: messenger, angel

exurgō (exsurgō), -ere, -rēxī: rise up

fāmen, -inis n.: utterance, speech

fungor, -ī, fūnctus sum (+abl.): perform, observe

gladius, -iī m.: sword

malefactum, -ī n.: evil deed

mendātium (CL: mendacium), -iī n.: lie

mentior, -īrī, mentītus sum: lie (about)

mūtus, -a, -um: silent, speechless

Orcus, -ī m.: the lower world; hell; god of the underworld

prīmō (adv.): at first, in the first place; at the beginning

prīnus, -ī f. (Grk. πρῖνος): holm oak tree

prōferō, -ferre, -tulī, -lātum: bring forth; make known, offer; utter

sānctus, -a, -um: venerable, holy

secō, -āre, -uī, sectum: cut

urgeō, -ēre, ursī: urge; press upon

vērum, -ī n.: truth

---

sānctus: the final syllable falls in the anceps position before the caesura

fāmine: abl. dependent on *fūnctus*

Quō: take *famine* as antecedent

prō crīmine: *instead of the accusation*

mentīris: the final syllable falls in the anceps position before the caesura

secet: jussive or optative subj.

Congaudēns ergō praesēns hōc cūria factō,   290
Rōre velut vellus, gaudet nimis ille popellus
Laudandō psallēns et gaudendō benedīcēns
Orbis factōrem, factīs semper meliōrem,
In sē spērantēs quī dat cito congratulantēs.

---

benedīcō, -ere, -dīxī, -dictum:
  commend, praise
congaudeō, -ēre, congāvīsus
  sum: rejoice together
cūria, -ae f.: senate; council
factor, -ōris m.: maker
maledīcō, -ere, -dīxī, -dictum:
  speak ill of, condemn
nimis (adv.): very much;
  exceedingly

popellus, -ī m.: crowd, mob
praesum, -esse, -fuī, -futūrum:
  be present
psallō, -ere, -ī: sing psalms
respondeō, -ēre, -ī, -sum:
  respond, answer
rōs, rōris m.: dew; moisture
vellus, -eris n.: fleece

---

hōc ... factō: abl. of cause

Rōre ... vellus: supply *esset*; *as if it were a fleece with dew*; a possible allusion to
  Judges 6:36-40, in which Gideon, a judge of Israel, tests God's will by asking him
  to miraculously wet a fleece with dew while leaving the ground dry

Laudandō, gaudendō: abl. gerunds used adverbially to express attendant
  circumstance, alongside present participles (*psallēns, benedīcēns*) (see section IV of
  the introduction for W.'s use of abl. gerunds)

In ... congratulantēs: see note on line 97

congratulantēs = *congrātulantēs*; W. treats the first *a* as short for the meter

Hinc in presbiterōs cōnsurgit plēbs moritūrōs,   295

Nam testēs falsōs Daniēl convīcerat ipsōs,

Quīs male reddēbant ut cognātae faciēbant:

Hōs et sorte parī dēcrēvērunt lapidārī.

Incidet in foveam, quisquis suffōderit illam.

Est etenim Chrīstus iūdex super omnia iūstus.   300

---

cognāta, –ae f.: relative (female)

cōnsurgō, –ere, –rēxī, –rēctum:
 rise together, rise up

convincō, –ere, –vīcī, –vīctum:
 prove wrong, convict

dēcernō, –ere, –crēvī, –crētum:
 decree; decide

falsus, –a, –um: deceptive, false

fovea, –ae f.: pit, ditch

incidō, –ere, –ī: fall into

iūdex, –icis m.: judge

lapidō (1): stone

pār, paris: equal

plēbs, plēbis f.: common people

reddō, –ere, didī, –ditum: return,
 pay back, punish

suffodiō, –ere, –fōdī, –fossum:
 dig

testis, testis m.: witness

Quīs = *Quibus*; dat. indirect object of *reddēbant*

Quīs … faciēbant: cf. Daniel 13:61: *fēcēruntque eīs sīcut male ēgerant adversus proximum* (*and they did to them just as they had wickedly done against their neighbor*)

faciēbant: conative imperf.: *they were trying to do*

Incidet … illam: cf. Proverbs 26:27: *Quī fodit foveam incidet in eam* (*He who digs a pit will fall into it.*)

Illā namque diē, quā dēbuit ipse perīre

Sanguis nōn meritus, homo tunc perit iste nocīvus.

Persōnīs trīnō laus, in deitāte sed ūnō,

Quod viget indempnis dēcēdēns hinc sine dampnīs

Ob meritum magna celebrī sub sorte Susanna.   305

---

celeber, –ebris, –ebre: renowned,
  famous

dampnum (CL: damnum), –ī
  n.: damage, injury

dēcēdō, –ere, –cessī, –cessum:
  withdraw, depart

deitās, –ātis f.: the divine nature,
  divinity

indempnis (CL: indemnis), –e:
  unhurt, unharmed

laus, laudis f.: praise, glory

meritus, –a, –um: deserving

nocīvus, –a, –um: hurtful,
  harmful

persōna, –ae f.: person, entity

trinus, –i, –ae: three each, triple

vigeō, –ēre, –uī: flourish, live

---

ipse: agrees with *Sanguis nōn meritus* (*undeserving blood,* i.e., innocent; referring to Susanna)

meritus: the final syllable falls in the anceps position before the caesura

homo = *homō*; **W.** treats the final *o* as short for the meter

[in] Personīs … ūnō: supply *sit*; *let there be praise to the three in person, but one in divinity*; a reference to the Christian concept of the Trinity

Quod: causal; *Susanna* is the postponed subject of *viget*

magna: the short nom. ending falls in the anceps position before the caesura

Susanna = *Sūsanna*; see note on line 16 of the prologue

Tū, pater Helchīa, vel māter, corde resultā
Et tibiīs ōdās vōbīs resonāte canōrās,
Quod Deus ēmundat, summum cui posse redundat,
Nātam dē scortō vel naevō crīminis ortō.
Inclite et ō Ioachim, manibus tū plaude diātim,   310
Coniuge prō lautā, magnīs virtūtibus auctā.

---

augeō, -ēre, auxī, auctum:
 honor, magnify
canōrus, -a, -um: tuneful,
 melodious
coniūnx, -iugis f.: spouse, wife
diātim (adv.): daily, every day
ēmundō (1): cleanse, purify
Helchīa, -ae m.: Helchia, father
 of Susanna
inclitus (inclutus), -a, -um:
 famous, renowned, magnificent
lautus, -a, -um: elegant,
 honorable

naevus, -ī m.: wart, stain
ōda, -ae f. (Grk. ᾠδή): ode, song
orior, -īrī, ortus sum: be born;
 rise
plaudō, -ere, plausī, plausum:
 clap, applaud
redundō (1): run over, overflow
resonō (1): resound, repeat
resultō (1): leap, ring, resound
scortum, -ī n.: fornication
tībia, -ae f.: pipe, flute

---

resultā, resonāte: imperatives
tibiīs = *tībiīs*; W. treats the first *i* as short for the meter
vōbīs: dat. of advantage
posse = *potestās*; modified by *summum*

Et cum cognātīs, cum cūnctīs vel tibi nōtīs,

Collaudā Dominum sollempnī vōce suprēmum,

Quod minus inventa rēs turpis cōnstat in illā,

Et Daniēl iūstus cūnctīs fuit inde probātus,   315

Quī senior mente datur atque prophēta repente.

Tunc populus reditū benedīxit tē, bone Iēsū,

Victrīcemque manum laudat, rēx optime rēgum,

Dēcantāns pariter mixtim cum dīvite pauper:

---

benedīcō, –ere, –dīxī, –dictum:
  commend, bless
cognātus, –ī m.: relative (male)
collaudō (1): praise very much,
  extol
cōnstō (1): stand, exist
dēcantō (1): sing repeatedly
minus (adv.): less; not so well; not
  quite
mixtim (adv.): mixedly, together
pauper, –eris: poor

prophēta, –ae m.: prophet
reditus, –ūs m.: return
repente: unexpectedly, suddenly;
  immediately
sollempnis (CL: sollemnis), –e:
  established, solemn
turpis, –e: repulsive, foul,
  shameful
victrīx, –īcis: victorious,
  triumphant

---

nōtīs: substantive: *friends*
Quod … illā: cf. Daniel 13:63: *quīa nōn esset inventa in eā rēs turpis*
inventa: the short nom. ending falls in the anceps position before the caesura
datur: *is made*
reditū: *in turn*

Ō quam mīra Deum testantur facta per aevum,   320

Cuius per nūtum reserat sapientia mūtum

Īnfantum linguās, cum vult, faciendo disertās,

Sīc dāns obscūra saepius mīrīfice clāra,

Quod die praesentī vīdērunt optime cūnctī,

In sē spērantem cum dat Deus īre iocantem.   325

---

disertus, -a, -um: clever, eloquent

Iēsūs, -ū m.: Jesus (Christ)

īnfāns, -antis: not capable of speech, speechless, not eloquent

iocor (1): jest, banter

Iēsūs –ū m.: Jesus (Christ)

lingua, -ae f.: speech, tongue

mīrificus, -a, –um: remarkable

mīrus, -a, –um: miraculous

mūtus, -a, –um: silent, speechless

nūtus, -ūs m.: nod, will

obscūrus, -a, -um: dark; obscure

optimus, -a, –um: best, excellent

praesēns, –entis: present, at hand

sapientia, -ae f.: wisdom

testōr (1): call upon, bear witness to

Cuius: take *Deum* as antecedent

Īnfantum linguās: direct object of *reserat*

faciendo: abl. gerund expressing means: *by making [them, i.e., infantum linguās] eloquent* (see section IV of introduction for W.'s use of abl. gerunds); W. treats the final *o* as short for the meter

dāns: *making*

obscūra: the short acc. ending falls in the anceps position before the caesura

saepius: comp. adv.; scans as two syllables

mīrīfice = *mīrificē*; W. treats the second *i* as long and the *e* as short for the meter

Quod: relative pronoun taking the previous clause as its antecedent

die, optime = *diē, optimē*; W. treats the *e* as short for the meter

In … iocantem: *when God grants the one trusting in Him to leave joyful*; a variation on a line repeated throughout the poem, cf. lines 97, 111, 187, 225, 294

Hinc laus aeterna rēgnāntī sorte paternā,

Glōria sit nātō genitōris mente creātō,

Spīrituī virtūs vigeat velut innuba myrtus,

Trīnae persōnae rēgnum deitātis honōre.

Sīc per saecla Deus, quī rēgnat trīnus et ūnus,   330

Sīc meritōs servat Deus et prāvōs male dampnat,

Virtūtis magnae ceu fēcerat huicque Susannae.

---

aeternus, -a, -um: everlasting

ceu: as, like

deitās, -ātis f.: the divine nature, deity

genitor, -ōris m.: father

honōs, -ōris m.: esteem, honor

innubus, -a, -um: unmarried, virgin

mereō, -ēre, -uī, -itum: deserve

myrtus, -ī m./f.: myrtle

paternus, -a, -um: paternal

persōna, -ae f.: person, entity

rēgnō (1): rule, reign

saeclum (saeculum), -ī n.: generation; age

trīnus, -a, -um: threefold, three

vigeō, -ēre, -uī: flourish, live

---

aeterna: the short nom. ending falls in the anceps position before the caesura

sit: jussive or optative subj. with both *laus* and *Glōria* as subjects

Spīrituī: dat. of advantage

vigeat: jussive or optative subj. with both *virtūs* and *rēgnum* as subjects

innuba myrtus: cf. Ovid's *Metamorphoses* 10.92: *innuba laurus*. Daphne was transformed into a laurel tree to escape Apollo's unwanted sexual advances, thus remaining *innuba*. In Christian symbolism, the myrtle can likewise represent virtue (cf. Isaiah 55:13: *prō urtīcā crēscet myrtus [instead of nettles a myrtle will grow]*).

Trīnae persōnae: *the Trinity*

Virtūtis magnae: gen. of description

huicque Susannae: dat. of advantage

Susannae = *Sūsannae*; see note on line 16 of the prologue

Ac, modo quod nōlim tantum, ceu fēcerat ōlim

Carcere submersō Iōsēph prō crīmine falsō,

Quī tunc īnsidiās malefīdē passus inīquās 335

Ēlēgit mortem mage quam mūtāre tenōrem,

Haec velutī casta luctāns cum sorte funestā,

Māluit ipsa morī quam tunc quid obēsse pudōrī.

---

carcer, -eris m.: jail, prison

castus, -a, -um: pure, chaste

ceu: as, like

ēligō, -ere, -lēgī, -lēctum: select, choose

falsus, -a, um: false

fūnestus, -a, -um: fatal, deadly

inīquus, -a, -um: uneven; unjust

īnsidiae, -ārum f. pl.: ambush, plot

Iōsēph (indeclinable): Joseph

lūctor (1): wrestle, struggle

mage (magis): more, rather

malefīdē: unfaithfully, faithlessly

obsum, -esse, -uī (+dat.): injure

ōlim (adv.): once, some time ago

patrōcinium, -iī n.: defense, protection

pudor, -ōris m.: shame, modesty

pūrus, -a, -um: pure, chaste

rīte: duly, correctly

submergō, -ere, -mersī, -mersum: submerge, plunge

tenor, -ōris m.: course, direction

---

modo … tantum = *tantummodo (only)*

Carcere submersō Iōsēph: rearrange: *Iōsēph submersō [in] carcere; submersō* agrees with indeclinable *Iōsēph*, a dat. of advantage with *fecerat*. In Genesis 39, Joseph is falsely accused of attempted rape and imprisoned after rejecting the sexual advances of Potiphar's wife.

casta: the short nom. ending falls in the anceps position before the caesura

funestā = *fūnestā*; W. treats the *u* as short for the meter

quid = *aliquid (in any way)*

Iōsēph namque virīs est ast miserēscere iūris

Rīte patrōciniō nec nōn vītāmine pūrō,   340

Nē male sēdūcī valeant aut dēnique vincī

Daemone discordī, quīs contīnentia cordī,

Quando pudītitiam petit ātra libīdo molestam.

āter, atra, atrum: black, dark

continentia, -ae f.: self-restraint

dēnique (adv.): finally, in the end

discors, -ordis: hostile

Iōsēph (indeclinable): Joseph

libīdo, -inis f.: desire, lust

miserēscō, -ere, —, —: feel pity, have compassion for (+gen.); have mercy on (ML: +dat./acc.)

molestus, -a, -um: distressed, troubled

pudītitia (CL: pudīcitia), -ae f.: chastity

Iōsēph: take as acc. subject of *miserēscere* after *est … iūris* (*it is right*; cf. line 39)

Iōsēph … iūris: *for it is also right for Joseph to take pity on men*

virīs: dat. dependent on *miserēscere*

ast = *at*; this word is our emendation for a second *est* (see Figure 12 and p. 27)

vītāmine = *vītā*

valeant: subj. in a negative purpose clause

quīs … cordī = *quibus continentia [est] [in] corde*

contīnentia = *continentia*; W. treats the first *i* as long for the meter

Quando = *Quandō*; W. treats the *o* as short for the meter

Figure 12. Detail from Bayerische Staatsbibliothek München, Clm 12513 (f. 31r).

Sīc quoque, Sūsanna, famulās miserando gubernā,

In tē mātrōnam quae spērant atque patrōnam,   345

Nē male sēdūcī valeāmus daemone trucī,

Quī nōs impugnat cupidus quō crīmine mergat,

---

cupidus, -a, -um: eager, greedy, lustful

famula, -ae f.: handmaiden; servant of God, i.e., nun

gubernō (1): steer, guide

impugnō (1): fight against, attack

mātrōna, -ae f.: matron, mother

mergō, -ere, mersī, mersum: immerse, plunge

miseror (1): pity, feel compassion for

patrōna, -ae f.: protectress, patroness

sēdūcō, -ere, -dūxī, -ductum: separate; lead astray

trux, trucis: wild, fierce

valeō, -ēre, -uī, -itum: be strong, be able

Sūsanna: the short vocative ending falls in the anceps position before the caesura

miserando: abl. gerund used adverbially to express manner or attendant circumstance (see section IV of the introduction for W.'s use of abl. gerunds); W. treats the *o* as short for the meter

valeāmus: subj. in a negative purpose clause

quō mergat = *ut mergat*; purpose clause

Ut bene tū nōstī, falsīs quia succubuistī,

Dōnec tē Chrīstus, iūdex super omnia iūstus,

Indignam sortis redimit sub tempore mortis,   350

Quī turbat nūllum, precibus quī commovet illum,

In sē spērantem sed dat cito congratulantem.

Quāpropter cūnctī Dominō servīre parātī,

Maxime vōs mātrēs, quae contempsistis amōrēs

**commoveō, -ēre, -mōvī,
-mōtum:** stir up, waken

**contempnō (CL: contemnō),
-ere, -tempsī, -temptum:** scorn,
avoid

falsum, -ī n.: untruth, falsehood

iūdex, -icis m.: judge

maximē: most greatly

quāpropter: for which reason

redimō, -ere, -dēmī, -demptum:
buy back; rescue

serviō, -īre, -īvī, -ītum (+dat.):
serve

**succumbō, -ere, -cubuī,
-cubitum (+dat.):** succumb to

turbō (1): disturb, confuse, distress

---

nōstī = *nōvistī*

sortis: gen. dependent on *Indignam*

sub ... mortis: *at the time of death*

Quī turbat: take *Chrīstus* as antecedent

quī commovet: take *nūllum* as antecedent

In ... congratulantem: *but swiftly makes the one trusting in Him thankful*; a
variation on a line repeated throughout the poem, cf. lines 97, 111, 187, 225, 294

congratulantem = *congrātulantem*; W. treats the first *a* as short for the meter

parātī: supply *sunt*

Maxime = *maximē*; W. treats the *e* as short for the meter

Et quās virgineō libuit rēgnāre trophaeō.   355

Cum mala vōs temptant vel iurgia daemonis īnstant

Dulcia, fallendō sīc, ad scelus illiciendō,

Hanc tunc victrīcem, vigilēs, attendite fortem,

Martiris ac magnae vel virginitātis alumpnae,

Intima cum tōtīs resonet vōx tunc prece vōtīs,   360

---

alumpna (CL: alumna), -ae f.:
  foster-daughter; pupil

attendō, -ere, -ī, -tentum:
pay attention (to), watch closely

fallō, -ere, fefellī, falsum:
  deceive; beguile

illiciō, -ere, -lēxī, -lectum:
  entice, seduce

īnstō, -āre, -stitī: threaten; insist
  upon

intimus, -a, -um: inmost

iurgium, -iī n.: altercation,
  quarrel

libet (libēre), libuit, libitum est:
  it pleases, it is agreeable

martir (martyr), -iris m./f.:
  martyr

rēgnō (1): rule, reign

resonō (1): resound

trophaeum, -ī n.: trophy

victrīx, -īcis f.: victor, fem.
  equivalent of *victor, -ōris*

vigil, -ilis: watchful, vigilant

virginitās, -ātis f.: virginity

virgineus, -a, -um: maidenly, of
  a virgin

---

quās: subject acc. of *rēgnāre*, inf. subject of impersonal *libuit*

Dulcia: substantive direct object of *īnstant*

fallendō, illiciendo: abl. gerunds used adverbially to express means (see section
  IV of the introduction for W.'s use of abl. gerunds); W. treats the *o* of *illiciendo*
  as short for the meter

vigilēs: voc. pl.

alumpnae: voc. pl.

resonet: jussive or optative subj.

prece: *in prayer*

Omnipotēns Chrīstus vestrōs ut dīrigat āctūs,

Ēripiēns vītās cōnservet et immaculātās,

Daemone dē dīrō necnōn temptāmine dūrō

Ob meritum magnae sub virginitāte Susannae,

Prō quā nunc praemium captāns conrēgnat in aevum   365

---

captō (1): grasp at, take, obtain

cōnservō (1): save; preserve

dīrigō (dērigō), –ere, –rēxī, –rēctum: direct, guide

dīrus, –a, –um: fearful, cruel

ēripio, –ere, –ui, –reptum: deliver, set free

immaculātus, –a, –um: unstained, pure

necnōn: and also, and yet

omnipotēns, –entis: all-powerful, almighty

praemium, –iī n.: prize, reward

rēgnō (1): rule, reign

spōnsa, –ae f.: betrothed, bride

temptāmen, –inis n.: trial

virginitās, –ātis f.: virginity

Omnipotēns ... āctūs: rearrange: *ut omnipotēns Chrīstus dīrigat vestrōs āctūs*; purpose clause

Susannae = *Sūsannae*; see note on line 16 of the prologue

Prō quā: take *virginitāte* as antecedent

praemium: scans as two syllables, the *i* is treated as a consonant

Sānctīs virginibus, quās dēspōnsāverat agnus,

Spōnsus, quī rēgnum spōnsīs dat dōte supernum,

Quī nōs perdūcat, quī sōlus cūncta gubernat.

Scrīptrīcī, magna, praemium tū ferto, Susanna,

Quae tibi sollempnem satagēbat dīcere laudem   370

Versibus hīs paucīs, incultīs ac male raucīs.

EXPLICIUNT VERSŪS WILLETRUDIS "DĒ SŪSANNĀ"

---

dēspōnsō (1): betroth, be espoused

dōs, dōtis f.: dowry

explicō (1): to unfold; complete, end

gubernō (1): steer, guide

incultus, -a, -um: unadorned, unpolished

laus, laudis f.: praise, glory

paucī, -ae -a: few

perdūcō, -ere, -dūxī, -ductum: lead

praemium, -iī n.: prize, reward

raucus, -a, -um: harsh, rough

sānctus, -a, -um: venerable, holy

satagō, -ere, -tēgī, -tāctum: strive for (+inf.), endeavor

scrīptrīx, -īcis f.: writer

sollempnis (CL: sollemnis), -e: established, customary

spōnsus, -ī m.: bridegroom

supernus, -a, -um: heavenly, celestial

versus, -ūs m.: line, verse

Sānctīs virginibus = *cum sānctīs virginibus*

dōte: *as a dowry*

perdūcat: subj. in place of expected ind. in order to rhyme with *gubernat*

magna: the short vocative ending falls in the anceps position before the caesura

praemium: scans as two syllables

ferto = *fertō*; W. treats the *o* as short; fut. active second person imperative

Susanna = *Sūsanna*; see note on line 16 of the prologue

Quae: take *Scrīptrīcī* as the antecedent

EXPLICIUNT: although *explicāre* is a first conjugation verb, the third plural form regularly appears as *expliciunt* (by analogy with *incipiunt*) at the end of works

Figure 13. A print by N. Braeu after a design by J. Matham, *Susanna in the bath*, c.1600. Rijksmuseum RP-P-BI-4269 / ArtStor.

This is the first translation of Willetrudis' work into any language. Because the purpose of this edition is to help readers understand Willetrudis' Latin, we hew very close to the phrasing of the original text, even when the result is awkward in English. In order to help readers easily flip between the Latin and English, each line in the English translation will correspond to the same numbered line in Latin, and the stanza breaks in English correspond to the page breaks in our edition of the Latin text.

SO BEGINS THE PROLOGUE OF WILLETRUDIS "ABOUT SUSANNA":

Although the deeds of the just have been more or less recorded
For the praise of their merit and for our consolation,
What benefit will there be in knowing, reader, or perhaps
    in desiring to know
In place of rumor (except the peace from these), if you do not rightly know
How to make use of following their example and also, in following,
    of imitating it?   5

The sure follower of these things will attain the reward.
Nevertheless, as I believe, no mere mortal here on earth
Whom either the strong deeds of God or the hour of the day warns,
While following brings to completion all those things yoked under the teachings
    of Christ.
Hence consider these words: we cannot all do all things.   10

But the one who strives more intently with their mind to ascend
The heights of virtue, in return for which the heights of salvation
    will be given,
He then especially pursues any just endeavors.
Anna had done this while Fenenna was bearing children,
Anna, who remained childless, until God increased her more.   15

And thus blesséd Susanna once upon a time strove for her reputation for chastity,
With which she struggled, until thereafter she was esteemed more.

Hence, having been warned, sisters, let it be pleasing to fortify
    your moral conduct
On the path of virtue, so that we do not hold on to a dangerous path
With weakened minds, but rather so that in worthy hymns   20
We may be found worthy of the Bridegroom, coming suddenly,

When He, having returned, cherishes his bride in the deep night.
Let us look to the shape of justice—as if for our own comfort—
Like to the shape of a mirror: uphold the standard.
Indeed the deeds of great Susanna must be imitated by us,   25
She who remained chaste under the force of the grievous skill of a demon.

Concerning her it has pleased my mind to create a pretty little book
    in verse,
Provided it is pleasing to Him thundering on high,
He who watches me crawling over my dactylic mistakes like a mouse.
And let Him arm me with His own strength   30
So that I may compose more readily, until I finally reach the end,
First through to the end, the same One who created the world.

SO BEGIN THE VERSES OF WILLETRUDIS "ABOUT SUSANNA":

Once upon a time, Babylon, famous for its power, flourished,
Which, by the standard of the times, was an ancient city,
Surpassing all cities which existed at that time,
Which, although the wealth of various riches
Had then shaped it to be the flourishing flower of the world,   5

Nevertheless that very city is said to have flourished still more
    with extraordinary men,
And indeed through the champions of the Lord and the sacred prophets,
As either the devout tradition proves, or this incident which is written down.
That so great a city was thus ennobled

With a joyful omen, in the age of a time now passed,   10
This is read in books, and at the same time is held to have been done in deeds.

Babylon once reared a distinguished citizen,
And this devout hero lived here, dwelling close to the city,
Ennobling the city, which he makes very famous throughout the world,
With his worthy and kind reputation, the reason for his esteem,   15
He surpasses the populace, and he is prominent because of his wealth.

And this man, noble and inclined towards every righteous thing
Is called Joachim, begotten of the highest stock.
This man deservedly brought upon himself the foremost honors
Among all his fellow-citizens, doing good deeds more readily.   20
Then beautiful Susanna married this man without derision,
Offspring of Helchia, born from the Judaean line.

And indeed such a maiden, to whom no other might compare,
Had these things fixed in her mind: always to serve the thundering one,
Just as maternal and paternal care instructs a daughter to do.   25
For they had been just, observing the commandments of Moses,
Esteemed parents, whom their blesséd daughter resembles.

Happy with this union and with such a wife,
This famous Joachim prevailed over each man in dignity
Since indeed he was wealthy and generous towards all.   30
Behold! There was an orchard near the house of this man,
To whom the Judaeans come, as do the Pharisees,
Because he is honored and esteemed before all.

Here, accustomed to renew the ancestral laws always,
At this time, the elders—alas! truly devoid of sense—   35
Are designated in pairs to govern the people,
About whom the Almighty warns us as follows, speaking thus:

Truly sin comes forth from the city of Babylon,
From the elders, for whom it is lawful to lay down the law for men
And by whom the people, if they are to be taught rightly,
    ought to be governed rightly.   40
And these men visited Joachim frequently, just as
    they were accustomed to before,
Around whom assembled all the people, to whom
    they pronounced judgment,
And this house of Joachim pronounces judgment to the people daily.

And when the people who had sought justice had returned home,
This remained the custom of Susanna at fixed times: 45
She enters the orchard, which by chance borders the house nearby,
And she bathes herself in the gentle waters of the fountain.
And as soon as the elders eagerly saw beautiful Susanna
Blooming, imbued in her face with golden color,

It occurred to them that this shining woman be united with them   50
In illicit sordid acts, and with the laws disregarded.
They were perverting their hearts, and were not looking to heaven
    in their minds,
And it pleases them least of all to remember God himself.
Finally, they were led astray, having agreed between themselves
    on its accomplishment,
As soon as they found the opportunity for this wicked deed.   55

They ready their ambush, and conceal themselves in the orchard,
Just as skilled as a fowler catches a turtle dove,
In the dark of a corner—who could believe this?—then
When indeed mistress Susanna with a springlike countenance,

A flowering lily, glowing in her rosy brightness,   60
Then accompanied by her handmaidens (just as she was accustomed),

Enters the orchard of her husband—since she wished to wash herself
     in the fountain,
For then the blazing heat was very troublesome—
Carefree—for what concern could she have there?

No one was here except the elders and herself,   65
And she did not sense the serpents cunningly hiding in the fountain,
With whose savage poisons she was about to be tainted
Just as Scylla long ago, whom the Greek myth describes,

Suffered the envy of cruel Circe, just like that of a stepmother,
When she bears upon her skin thousands upon thousands of blemishes.   70
What reason is there then for the men, or what intent for passion,
When they, alone, had seen her, alone, about to wash herself
     in the fountain?
For she, about to bathe, orders the two handmaidens by whom
     she was accompanied
Where they should carry the soaps and from there to leave straightaway.

Saying, "I want to wash in the fountain. Close the doors of the orchard   75
Behind you, and also hasten to return back."
And they, having departed, soon complete the task they were ordered
     to do there.
How naive to deceit and how unaware of your fate you had been,
Worthy of your father, a dove who endures such extremes of deceit.

And just like a swan—or what is better: a tender lamb!—   80
And just like a swan, whom a kite follows to seize,
Or a tender lamb, running along, whom a wolf seizes unexpectedly,
You are held in the mouth of the wolf or you will be held in the beak
     of the kite,
But you, perhaps, will be ravaged by the wolf and the kite
     at the same time,

While you were here alone, the patroness to be remembered for the ages,   85
A champion of the Lord. Behold, the elders, whom their own wantonness

Had made worthless slaves to serve blind Orcus here on earth,
Perverting their own reason through wanton desire,
Accosted pious Susanna, whom they strongly desired
At the wall of the orchard, where they wished to be hidden,   90
As the wolf himself is accustomed to do, to whom the lamb
    by chance has run.
What emotion had there been, or what sort was your impulse,
O venerable woman of God, when you realized you were being touched
    wrongly by these men?

What groans should you give, or what kind of gestures with your body,
When you were naked, trembling from fear among thieves?   95
But your mind was fixed, trusting in the kindly Lord,
Who swiftly makes those trusting in Him thankful,
And the conspirators evilly utter their own wish,
And with such a voice, they attempt to persuade her to fornicate:
"Yield to our desire, so that we may remain beloved to you.   100
Everything is secure: indeed, the doors have been barred.
Now do not delay, but indeed by our pledge of love
Be joined with us willingly. What's more, if, unwilling,
You should denounce us, soon thereafter you would be stoned."

O, the evil and quick agreement of both these men,   105
Which they together attempted to set in motion quite wickedly.
Forever blind to the merits of worthy and holy Susanna,
Likewise they remained fixed in their very persistent request,
But that immovable woman, not inclined towards the offers of these men,
Endures, placing her hope in the foremost Lord on high,   110
Who swiftly makes those trusting in Him thankful.

Thus also, then not having obtained the fulfillment of their evil deed,

They resort to alternate weapons with viperous venoms,
And say with a wicked voice these things, namely, this speech.
Here and now is the offense: "Do as our order wishes,   115
Because if you object, perhaps you will be troubled by falsehoods.
We will say that we saw a young man flirting with you,
And that for this reason, you sent the two handmaidens from here."

Susanna, who must be remembered by all as a worthy example,
Cornered at a crossroads, since she was struck by the bite of accusation,   120
Groans from the heart, pouring these words so sweetly from her mouth:
"I am completely cornered and unsure of what I should do first;
If by chance I do this, I destroy myself with an eternal death;
Nor will I escape your perverse hands, if I refuse.
But, for me, let it be preferable that I reject your desire   125
Rather than sinfully submit myself to your offer."

Already grieving more inside, not wanting to succumb to wickedness,
Then blesséd Susanna cries out with a great voice indeed,
And the very wicked men cry out together against the pious woman.
Dark lust was fighting with a faithful heart.   130
Now, with prayers poured forth, I will grant to you, Muses, to say
What kind of conflicts virtue waged with accusation,
Or how evils fell upon the immense spear of virtue.
And reveal outwardly what desire burned within.

Then one of them swiftly and vigorously unbars the doors   135
And the house servants of Joachim, and likewise the servants of the elders,
Rush through the back doors, they seek what the cause is
Of such a great outcry, which all had heard there.

The elders say that they saw a young man flirting with her,
With the mistress caught in the act, and by this unspeakable utterance   140
They were then struck deep in their hearts, because nowhere
    had they heard

The blow of such a deed spoken about this venerable wife.

Ah, ah, Rumor, than whom no evil is swifter,
Flies around and at once makes the matter known far and wide.
She bears as many falsehoods as Scylla does blemishes,   145
And this charge of adultery makes the relatives of this woman,
Who inwardly lament, sorrowful, convene from every quarter,

And indeed the kindly people, considering everything,
Were assembling before these men, whom they held in higher esteem,
Of one mind, mixed together, the poor man with the rich man.   150
Both men excelled in zeal, more worthy than all others.

Naturally, all her relatives were won over to them,
And her faithful fellow citizens straightaway were in agreement with them
What it meant, many for whom this matter grieves them in the heart.

Behold! First thing on the following day, it is settled in this manner: 155
The people, the arbiter of this accusation, assemble
And one by one a crowd amasses in the home of Joachim.
They arrive, depraved and full of depraved thought,
The two elders, stripping their words of truth,
Who say to the people, summoned by their orders: 160

"Send forth Susanna, whom we know, ah, unworthy
as the spouse of Joachim, she whom we once cherished.
Summon the daughter of Helchia to be put to death
    according to the laws."
And soon they sent for and thus summoned forth Susanna,
Who, fully fortified by hope in the Lord and not delaying at all,   165
Praying with psalms, accompanied by her blesséd parents,
And with all her relatives and friends,
She hastens quite readily, and at once she arrived here and enters.

All weep for her, whoever had known her.
Here also, the elders, for whom it is law within the Law to revere   170
The Lord enthroned on high, although by them badly scorned then,
Ordered that the clothes be stripped from her delicate body,

And with their gaze, they violate the private parts of worthy Susanna,
So that a corrupted mind might be satisfied by the sight.
O, grossly perverted men, turned worse after worst,   175
What were you thinking, looking upon the nude body of this woman?
And isn't it better to live, if the mind should avoid perceiving these things?
It does not shame her, that with which the Maker clothes any mortal.

In that which nature gave, anyone will have enough.
What should I say to you to condemn a sinful mind?   180
Let there soon be hellfire for you as your just deserts!
Then side by side they rise, as they proceed to state their case
For they have sat down among the people on their curule chair,
And they place their hands above her head while swearing an oath.

And she, weeping very much, was endeavoring to look to heaven,   185
And her heart was trusting deeply in Christ the Lord,
Who swiftly makes those trusting in Him thankful.
But the judges, having turned, spoke, beginning in this way:
"By chance, yesterday, when we walked alone
In this man's orchard, which lies near his home, then   190
This woman had come accompanied only by two handmaidens,

And straightaway, dismissing her handmaidens with a word,
She ordered that the gates of the orchard be barred with a bolt.
Thereupon, bursting forth, a youth had embraced her,
Which we saw, hidden by chance nearby.   195
With a hurried pace, soon we both approached that place.
When we arrived, we see that they were already consorting.

Meanwhile, the youth, swiftly opening the gates then,
We are not able to seize, for being stronger than us he slipped away.
And indeed, after she was apprehended, we interrogate her:
    "Say who the man is!"   200
And she, questioned and denying, steadfastly refuses to utter these things.
Indeed, we are faithful witnesses in our account of this matter."

Therefore, with these things said, the people soon believed those men
As elders, mature in judgment and supposedly in their conduct.
For sorrow! They wickedly decreed this fate, death, for her,   205
But fortune does this more than You do, God of the world;
While You lived in the flesh, You too were subjected to fortune,
By tasting death, restoring salvation to all.

O evil fortune, never remaining under a single lot,
But bending all things and overwhelming everything powerful,   210
High or low, You always make them take part in your games,
Not having deigned to spare even worthy Susanna,
Whom, most innocent, you now contrived to be guilty.

And Susanna, weeping and sighing deeply, had said:
"O Eternal God, highest ruler in the heights   215
Of the heavenly palace, and You, blesséd founder of the world,
Knower of hidden things, likewise glorious maker of the universe,
God, fully knowing all things before they happen.

You know, O Lord, that a falsehood is hurled against me,
Behold, indeed, I am ruined, and I will be wrongfully deprived of life,   220
Doing none of these things, nor having knowledge of these inventions."
She invokes this name — how great an omen may it bring!
And God mercifully heard her voice from on high,

As a merciful supporter and equally a lover of salvation,
Who swiftly makes those trusting in Him thankful.   225

Anyone on Earth is able to look upon His heavenly power,
Anyone of an afflicted heart, or the pious voice of a pure mind
Or if someone is touched or beset by unjust troubles.

How swiftly may He extend His eternal ears all the way,
About whom the singer of psalms, proclaiming, added these things: 230
"O God, You do not reject a humbled and initiated heart
And a spirit in tribulation remains pleasing to you."

Contemplating which proverb in her mind, worthy Susanna
Very humbled and afflicted, calls upon You, God,
She whom You mercifully hear, benevolent God of the world,   235
You who prefer that one be struck by a whip and condemned by You.

Susanna is led to her death accompanied by the whole crowd,
Fulfilling martyrdom in her mind and in her remaining life,
Forever worthy under a famous fate.
But the Spirit of the Lord then flowed into a young boy,   240
Who had made his age full of judgment,
Who was called Daniel, crying out only once,
And he had uttered this phrase clearly drawn forth by divine inspiration:

"Behold, I am innocent of the condemnation of this woman's blood."
All listened to this utterance as though stunned,   245
And the whole crowd, as if one, responded this to him:
"Where are these words which you speak going, then, boy?"
Then, standing in their midst, Daniel said with his virtuous mouth:

"O children of Israel, here it is evident that you are slow to understand,
Crooked in your judgment, with no discernment of the truth.   250
How badly you now condemn a daughter of Israel on behalf of those men,
Although the people, whom this trial moves, may now gather here
in order to condemn both those elders."
At once, turned around, they sit down where they were ordered.

And now Daniel, upon whom the Spirit drips this honey, says: 255

"Let those involved in the accusation be set far apart,
Until I prove the crooked madness of their thinking."
And they were soon separated and no longer dared to mumble.
When one was brought forth, Daniel spoke to him thus:

"You, already ancient villain, inveterate source of evils,   260
The things which you, sinful, did before will catch up to you,
Condemning the innocent, and acquitting the guilty,
Although God, whom the heavenly order serves, says thus
That no just innocent be put to death with you as judge.

Now, if you did see, say openly what you know well: 265
Under which tree did you see them speaking with each other?"
And he, quickly responding, had boldly said: "Under a mastic tree."
And righteous Daniel, to whom Christ dictates these few words:
"Because you lie about this, you will die and go to Orcus.
Behold, an angel of God, beating you with the whip of truth,   270
Will rip you in half, balancing this deed against you."

Thus, most thoroughly convicted, that man soon was taken away.
When the other was brought forth, Daniel spoke to him thus:
"You, seed of Canaan and descendant betraying Judah
    for your own benefit,
Badly has beauty beguiled you and virtue left you,   275
And perverted your senses with wanton lust.

Thus you were treating the daughters of Israel everywhere,
Who, exceedingly scared out of their wits, all were speaking with you.
But a daughter of Judah never submitted to those evils.
Because you said these things, say openly what you know well: 280
Under which tree, good sir, did you apprehend them?"

Saying, "Under the oak tree," he utters lies,
At first feeling safe with the oak tree, intending to remain silent to the end.
Then this holy boy, having observed the testimony of both men,
By which the truth in place of the accusation becomes very clear to all,   285
Responding clearly, bitterly rebuked this man thus:
"Because you lie about these things, you will die and go to Orcus.
Let a just angel rising up, pressing upon you more justly,
Cut your very self in half with a sword for this evil deed."

Thus the present council, rejoicing together at this deed,   290
As if it were a fleece with dew, that crowd rejoices exceedingly,
Praising and singing psalms, rejoicing and blessing
The creator of the world, always better by His deeds,
Who swiftly makes those trusting in Him thankful.

At this point the people rise up against the elders condemned to die,   295
For Daniel had convicted them as false witnesses,
Whom they severely punished just as they were trying to do to their relative:
And with an equal fate they condemned them to be stoned.
Whoever digs a pit will fall into it.
For truly Christ is a righteous judge over all things.   300

For indeed on that day, on which undeserving blood itself
was due to die, that malignant man then died.
Let there be praise to the three in person, but one in divinity,
Because, departing from here unharmed, without injury,
Under a famous fate, great Susanna survives on account of her merit.   305

You, father Helchia, and her mother, resound with your heart
And with your flutes ring out melodious songs for yourselves,
Because God, for whom the highest power abounds, purifies
His daughter of fornication and the stain sprung from the accusation.
And you, O renowned Joachim, applaud with your hands every day   310
For your honorable wife, magnified by her great virtues.

And with your relatives and all your friends,
Praise the highest Lord with a solemn voice,
Because this shameful deed is no longer found in her,
And Daniel was from then on deemed just by all,   315
Who is made older in his mind and a prophet all at once.
Then the people blessed you in turn, good Jesus,
And praise your triumphant hand, best king of kings,
Singing together, the poor mixed together with the rich:

O, how miraculous deeds bear witness to God through the ages,   320
Through whose silent nod wisdom unlocks
the tongues of the speechless, when He wants, by making them eloquent,
Thus making obscure things quite often remarkably clear,
Which on the present day all saw perfectly,
When God grants the one trusting in Him to leave joyful.   325

Hence may there be eternal praise to the one ruling by paternal destiny,
May there be glory to the Son of the Father, created in His mind,
May virtue flourish for the Spirit, just as the virgin myrtle,
May the kingdom of the Trinity flourish with the honor of divinity.
Thus, through the ages, God, who rules as three and one,   330
Thus God saves the deserving and severely condemns the wicked,
Just as He had done for this Susanna, a woman of great virtue.

And also (but which I wouldn't wish for) just as He had done once
For Joseph, cast into prison for a false charge,
Who then, having suffered faithlessly unjust treacheries,   335
Chose death rather than to change his course,
As this chaste woman, struggling with a deadly fate,
Herself preferred to die than to do injury to her modesty in any way.

For indeed it is also right for Joseph to have pity on men
Justly by patronage and also with a pure life,   340

So that they can't be badly led astray or ultimately vanquished
By a discordant demon, for whom there is restraint in their heart,
When dark lust attacks troubled modesty.

So too, Susanna, with compassion guide your handmaidens,
Who trust in you as a matron and a patroness,   345
So that we can't be badly led astray by a fierce demon,
Who, desirous, assails us, so that he might immerse us in sin,

As you well know, because you fell victim to falsehoods,
Until Christ, the righteous judge over all things,
Rescues you, unworthy of your fate, at the time of death,   350
He who distresses no man who moves Him with prayers,
But swiftly makes the one trusting in Him thankful.
For which reason all are ready to serve the Lord,
Especially you, mothers, who have scorned love affairs

And whom it pleased to reign with the trophy of virginity.   355
When evils tempt you and a demon's quarrels urge
Sweet things, thus deceiving and seducing you into sin,
Then, watchful, fix your attention on this strong victrix,
You pupils of the great martyr and of virginity,
Then let your inmost voice resound in prayer with all your vows,   360

So that all powerful Christ may guide your actions,
And deliver and preserve your pure lives
From a cruel demon and also a difficult temptation
Because of the merit of great Susanna embodied in her virginity,
On account of which now receiving her reward she rules with Him
     for eternity   365

With her holy virgins, to whom the Lamb, the Bridegroom, is betrothed,
Who gives His heavenly kingdom to His brides as a dowry,
Who leads us, who alone governs all things.

Great Susanna, bring forth a reward for the writer,
Who was striving to speak solemn praise for you   370
With these few verses, unadorned and very rough.

SO END THE VERSES OF WILLETRUDIS "ABOUT SUSANNA"

GLOSSARY

ā: ah!

ā/ab/abs (+abl.): (away) from; by (agency)

āctus, -ūs m.: act, action; impulse

ad (+acc.): toward, to; for the purpose or benefit of; to suit

addō, -ere, -didī, -ditum: to give to; to add, say in addition; increase

adsum, adesse, -fuī, -futūrus: to be present

adversus (+acc.): facing, opposite, against, opposed (to)

aevum, -ī n.: generation, age; eternity

afflīgō, -ere, -īxī, -īctum: to beat, strike, crush

agnus, -ī m.: lamb

agō, -ere, ēgī, āctum: to drive; do; spend, conduct; concern oneself with; make a proposal (about)

āiō: to say, assert

almus, -a, -um: blesséd, kind

alter, altera, alterum: the other (of two)

altus, -a, -um: tall, high; deep

ambō, -ae, -ō: both

amō (1): to love

amor, -ōris m.: love

ante: before, earlier, previously; in front of (+acc.)

arbor, -oris f.: tree

arma, -ōrum n.: arms, weapons

ars, artis f.: skill, art; talent; guile, trick

at (ast): but, but on the other hand; on the contrary; while, whereas; but yet; at least

atque (ac): and in addition, or and besides; and, as well, and indeed

audeō, -ēre, ausus sum: to dare

audiō, -īre, -īvī, -ītum: to hear, listen (to)

auris, auris f.: ear

aut: or

aut…aut: either…or

bene: well

bonus, -a, -um: good

cadō, -ere, cecidī, cāsum: to fall, sink; die, be killed; derive from, proceed from (a source)

caput, -itis n.: head

causa, -ae f.: reason, cause; case; lawsuit

cēdō, -ere, cessī, cessum: to go, move; yield; withdraw

cernō, -ere, crēvī, certum: distinguish, discern, see; resolve, determine; decree

certus, -a, -um: sure, certain, reliable; fixed; resolved, determined

cito (adv.): quickly

cīvis, cīvis m./f.: citizen

clārus, -a, -um: bright, clear; famous, distinguished

claudō, -ere, clausī, clausum: to close, shut, block up; confine

clēmēns, -entis: merciful

cognōscō, -ere, -nōvī, -nitum: to come to know, learn, recognize; (in perf.) know

color, -ōris m.: color, shade; quality

comitō (1): to accompany, follow

congrātulor (1): congratulate, rejoice, give thanks

conregnō (1): to reign together with one

cōnsequor, cōnsequī, cōnsecūtus sum: to follow, go/come after; overtake; attain

cor, cordis n.: heart

corpus, -oris n.: body

crēdō, -ere, -didī, -ditum: to trust, believe (+dat.); entrust

creō (1): produce, beget, create

crīmen, -inis n.: verdict, accusation

cum: when (+ indic.); since (+ subjunctive); although (+ subjunctive)

cum (+abl.): with

cūnctus, -a, -um: all, entire; all together

cupiō, -ere, -īvī/-iī, -ītum: to wish/be eager for; desire, want; favor

cūra, -ae f.: care, concern; anxiety

daemōn, -onis m.: spirit, demon

dampnō (CL: damnō) (1): find guilty, condemn

dē (+abl.): down from, about, concerning; starting at (a point in time)

dēbeō, -ēre, -uī, dēbitum: to owe; ought

deus, -ī m.: god

dīcō, -ere, dīxī, dictum: to say, speak, tell

dictum, -ī n.: word; saying

diēs, -ī m./f.: day

dīgnus, -a, -um: worthy; (+abl.) worthy (of)

dīves, -itis: rich, wealthy

dō, dare, dedī, datum: to give; dedicate; sell; pay; grant, lend; devote; allow; make

doceō, -ēre, -uī, doctum: to teach, show, point out

dolor, -ōris m.: pain, grief, sorrow

domina, -ae f.: mistress of the family, wife; lady

domus, -ī f.: house, home

dōnec: while; until

dūcō, -ere, dūxī, ductum: to lead; consider

dulcis, -e: sweet, pleasant

dum: while, as long as, until; provided that; since

duō, duae, duo: 2

dūrus, -a, -um: hard, harsh

ecce: lo! behold! look!

efficiō, -ere, effēcī, effectum: to make; carry out, accomplish; bring about

egō, meī, mihi, mē, mē: I; me

enim: in fact, indeed; for

eō, īre, -īvī/-iī, itum: to go, walk; pass

ergō: therefore; well, then, now

et: and

etenim: and indeed; for in fact

ex (ē) (+abl.): out of, from

faciēs, -eī f.: appearance, face, form

faciō, -ere, fēcī, factum: to make; do; reckon

factum, -ī n.: deed

fāma, -ae f.: report, rumor; reputation, fame; tradition, story

fēlīx, fēlīcis: fortunate, happy

ferō, ferre, tulī, lātum: to bring, bear, carry; endure

fīlia, -ae f.: daughter

fīnis, fīnis m.: boundary, end, limit; (pl.) country, territory, land

fīō, fierī, factus sum: to become; happen, result, occur

fleō, -ēre, flēvī, flētum: to cry for; cry, weep

fōns, fontis m.: spring, fountain, well, source

fōrma, -ae f.: shape, form, appearance; beauty; mold, pattern

fors, fortis f.: chance, luck

forte: by chance

fortis, -e: brave; strong

fortūna, -ae f.: chance, luck

fugiō, -ere, fūgī, -itum: to flee, escape; avoid (+inf.)

gaudeō, -ēre, gāvīsus sum: to be glad, rejoice

gerō, -ere, gessī, gestum: to bear; manage, conduct; perform

glōria, -ae f.: renown, glory

grātus, -a, -um: pleasant; grateful

habeō, -ēre, -uī, habitum: to have, hold; consider

hic, haec, hoc: this, these

hinc: from here, hence; henceforth

hōc: to this place

homō, -inis m.: human being, man; (pl.) people

honōrus, -a, -um: honorable; glorifying

iaciō, -ere, iēcī, iactum: to throw, hurl, cast; throw away; utter

iam: now; already

ibī: in that place, there; then, thereupon

īdem, eadem, idem: same

igitur: therefore

ignis, ignis m.: fire

ille, illa, illud: that; those

illō (illōc): to that place, thither

impōnō, -ere, -pōsuī, -pōsitum: to impose; establish; inflict; assign; deceive, impose upon (+dat.)

in (+abl.): on

in (+acc.): into, onto; against

incipiō, -ere, -cēpī, -ceptum: to begin

inde: from that place, from there, thence; from that time, thereupon

indīgnus, -a, -um: unworthy (of) (+ abl./gen.); whom it does not befit (+ inf.)

inquam, inquis, inquit, inquiunt: to say; it is said

intentē: intently

inter (+acc.): between, among; during

inveniō, -īre, -vēnī, -ventum: to find, discover

Iōsēph (indeclinable): Joseph

ipse, ipsa, ipsum: himself/herself/itself (intensive); very

is, ea, id: he/she/it; that

Isrāel (indeclinable): Israel

iste, ista, istud: that (of yours); those (of yours)

ita: in this way, so, thus

iubeō, -ēre, iussī, iussum: to order, tell, command, direct; decree

Iūdaea, -ae f.: Judea

iūs, iūris n.: right, justice, law; legal system; code; duty; court; binding decision; oath

iūstitia, -ae f.: righteousness, justice, equity

iūstus, -a, -um: just, righteous

iuvō (1): to help; please

laudō (1): to praise

lavō (1): wash, bathe

legō, -ere, lēgī, lēctus: to choose, collect; read

lēx, lēgis f.: law

locus, -ī m.: place, region, part; passage (in a piece of writing)

longus, -a, -um: long, far

loquor, loquī, locūtus sum: to speak

magnus, -a, -um: large, big; great; mighty; distinguished;
  notable/famous

mālō, māluī, mālle: want more; prefer

malus, -a, -um: bad, evil

maneō, -ēre, mānsī, mānsum: to remain, stay; await; wait for;
  continue, endure, last

manus, -ūs f.: hand; band of men

māter, mātris f.: mother

mātūrus, -a, -um: ripe, mature

melior, -ius: better

mēns, mentis f.: mind; intention, purpose; attitude

meritum, -ī n.: a thing deserved, desert; service, reward, merit,
  value

mīlle: thousand

mittō, -ere, mīsī, missum: to send; release, let go; omit, leave off
  (+ inf.)

modo: provided that; only, just; now, just now

mollis, -e: flexible; mild; easy; calm; weak; cowardly; unmanly;
  tender (women/youths)

morior, morī, mortuus sum: to die

mors, mortis f.: death

mōs, mōris m.: custom, practice, habit; mood, manner, fashion; character (pl.), behavior, morals

moveō, -ēre, mōvī, mōtum: to move

mox: soon; then

multus, -a, -um: much, many

mūtō (1): to change

nam: for

nāscor, nāscī, nātus sum: to be born, come into being, be formed

nāta, -ae f.: daughter

nātūra, -ae f.: nature

nātus, -a, -um: born, descended

nātus, -ī m.: son; (pl.) children

nē: not; in order that…not; that…not; that

negō (1): to deny, refuse; say…not

neque (nec): and not; neither…nor

nihil (nīl) n.: nothing

nisi (nī): if…not, unless

nōlō, nōlle, nōluī: to be unwilling, not want, not wish (+ inf.)

nōmen, -inis n.: name

nōn: not

nōnne: introduces a direct question expecting the answer "yes"

nōs, nostrum/nostrī: we, us

nōscō, -ere, nōvī, nōtum: to come to know, learn, recognize; (perf.) know; become familiar with; examine, study, inspect; try (case); accept as true; recall

noster, nostra, nostrum: our(s)

nōtus, -a, -um: well-known, familiar, notable, famous

nox, noctis f.: night

nūllus, -a, -um: not any, no

num: introduces a direct question expecting the answer "no"; (introduces an indirect question) whether

numquam: never

nunc: now

ō: O

ob (+acc.): on account of, because of

omnis, -e: every; all

oppidum, -ī n.: town

optimus –a –um: best

orbis, orbis m.: circle, orb; a circular path, circuit; the world

ōs, ōris n.: mouth; face

ōstium (ML: hōstium), -iī n.: gate, door; entrance

parēns, -ntis m./f.: parent

pariter: likewise, at the same time; alike

parō (1): to prepare; provide; produce; obtain; buy; raise; plan

pater, patris m.: father

patior, patī, passus sum: to experience, suffer, endure; permit, allow

pāx, pācis f.: peace; favor

pectus, -oris n.: chest, breast; heart

per (+acc.): through

pereō, -īre, -iī, -itūm: to perish, die; be destroyed

perveniō, -īre, -vēnī, -ventum: to come to; reach; arrive

petō, -ere, -īvī/-iī, -ītum: to ask for, seek; attack; make for, go towards

pius, -a, -um: dutiful, loyal; sacred; merciful (when applied to God or Christ) placeō, -ēre, -uī, placitum: to be pleasing, please (+dat.)

plēnus, -a, -um: full

plūs, plūris n.: more

pōmērium (CL: pōmārium), -iī n.: garden

pōnō, -ere, posuī, positum: to put, place; set aside; lend (money)

populus, -ī m.: (the) people

possum, posse, potuī: to be able, can

post: after(ward), later; behind (+acc.)

potestās potestātis f.: power, rule, force; strength, ability; chance, opportunity

praeclārus, -a, -um: very clear; bright

prāvus, -a, -um: crooked, perverse

prespiter (CL: presbyter), -erī m.: elder

prex, precis f.: prayer, request

prīmum: first; for the first time

prīmus, -a, -um: first, foremost, best, chief, principal

prō (+abl.): on behalf of, for, instead of, in accordance with; in order to

probō (1): test, prove; approve, esteem; attest

puella, -ae f.: girl

puer, -ī m.: boy

pulcher, pulchra, pulchrum: beautiful, handsome

putō (1): to think, suppose

quālis, quāle: what sort of; of which sort, as

quam: than; as, how; (+ superlative) as…as possible

quamvīs: even though, although, however you like; altogether

quandō: when, since, because

quī, quae, quod: who, which, that

quia: because

quidem: moreover, certainly

quis, quid: who, what

quisquam, quicquam: someone, something; anyone, anything

quisque, quidque/quīcque: each, every; each one, every one, everything

quisquis, quidquid/quicquid: whoever, whichever

quō: where; to what purpose, what for; on account of which; so that; in order that; (expresses degree of difference)

quod: because

quoque: also, too

quot: how many, as many as

referō, referre, rettulī, relātum: to bring back; report

rēgnum, -ī n.: royal power; power; control; kingdom

relinquō, -ere, relīquī, relictum: to leave (behind), abandon

reserō (1): open, reveal, expose

resultō, -āre, —, resultātum: to leap back/again, rebound; reverberate, resound

rēx, rēgis m.: king

saepe: often

saevus, -a, -um: cruel, savage

sānctus, -a, -um: venerable, holy

sanguis, -inis m.: blood

sānus, -a, -um: sound; healthy; sensible; sane

satis (sat): enough

scelus, -eris n.: wicked deed, crime, sin

scīlicet (adv.): certainly, that is to say

scio, -īre, -īvī/iī, -ītum: to know

scrībō, -ere, scrīpsī, scrīptum: to write

sed: but

sēdulus, -a, -um: careful, cautious, purposeful; diligent, zealous

semper: always

senex, senis m.: elder

sēnsus, -ūs m.: perception, feeling; sense

sentiō, -īre, sēnsī, sēnsum: to perceive; feel

sequor, sequī, secūtus sum: to follow; come next

servus, -ī m.: enslaved person

sī: if

sīc: thus, so, in this way, in such a way

simul: at same time; likewise; also; simultaneously; at once

simulō (1): to imitate, copy; pretend (to have/be); look like;
 simulate; counterfeit; feint

sine (+abl.): without

solitus, -a, -um: having been accustomed

sōlus, -a, -um: alone, only

soror, -ōris f.: sister

sors, sortis f.: lot, fate

spectō (1): to look at, observe

spērō (1): to hope, believe, trust

spēs, speī f.: hope

spīritus, -ūs m.: breath, spirit; the Holy Spirit

stō, -āre, stetī, statum: to stand; stand fast, endure

sub (+abl.): under; at the foot of; near; up to

subsanno (1): to insult by derisive gestures, to deride, mock

suī, sibi, sē, sē: himself/herself/itself (reflexive)

sum, esse, fuī, futūrus: to be; exist

summus, -a, -um: highest; top (of); last, final

super: above, on top, over; upwards; moreover, in addition, besides; during (time)

suprēmus -a -um: highest

suus, -a, -um: his/her/its own; their own

tālis, -e: such, of such a sort

tam: so

tamen: nevertheless, however

tangō, -ere, tetigī, tāctum: touch, strike, reach; mention

tantus, -a, -um: so much, so great, of such size

tempus, -oris n.: time

teneō, -ēre, -uī, tentum: to hold, grasp; keep, possess; occupy

tener, tenera, tenerum: tender

tentō (1): to try, test

ternī, -ae, -a: three each

tot: so many

tōtus, -a, -um: whole

tū, tuī, tibi, tē, tē: you

tum (tunc): then, at that time

turba, -ae f.: crowd, uproar

tūtus, -a, -um: safe, prudent; secure; protected

tuus, -a, -um: your, yours

ubī: where; when

ūllus, -a, -um: any

ulterior, -ius: farther

ultimus, -a, -um: farthest, latest; last; highest, greatest

ūnus, -a, -um: one, alone; single

urbs, urbis f.: city

ut (utī): to, in order to (+ subj.); how, when, as (+ indic.)

ūtor, ūtī, ūsus sum: to use; (+abl.) experience, enjoy

vel: or; either…or; even

velut (velutī): even as, just as, like as, like

veniō, -īre, vēnī, ventum: to come

verbum, -ī n.: word

vērō: certainly, in truth, in fact, truly

vertō, -ere, -ī, versum: to turn, turn around; change; overthrow, destroy

vērus, -a, -um: real, true

vester, vestra, vestrum: your (pl.), yours (pl.)

vestis, vestis f.: garment, clothing; clothes

videō, -ēre, vīdī, vīsum: to see; (passive) be seen, seem

vincō, -ere, vīcī, victum: to conquer, overcome

vir, -ī m.: man

virgō, -inis f.: maiden, young woman; virgin

virtūs, -tūtis f.: manliness, courage; excellence, virtue

vīs, vis f.: force, power; violence; (pl.) physical strength

vīta, -ae f.: life

vīvō, -ere, vīxī, vīctum: to live

vocō (1): to call; summon; name

volō, velle, voluī: to be willing, want, wish; mean, signify

voluntās voluntātis f.: desire

vōs, vestrum/vestrī: you (plural)

vōtum, -ī n.: solemn promise, vow; hope

vōx, vōcis f.: voice; word